The End
of Small Groups

LEADING INCARNATIONAL VILLAGES

DARYL L. SMITH

Don·Q·Dox

THE END of Small Groups
Leading Incarnational Villages

© 2015 by Daryl L. Smith

Offered by Don•Q•Dox (www.DonQDox.com)

Design and layout: Carolyn B. Smith

ISBN: 978-0-6924-6231-7

Dedicated to...
Al Turner
who introduced me to my first small group;
Spring Arbor College *(University) Life Team*
that taught me how to live in a vulnerable community;
Faith At Work *(now Lumunos)*
the ministry that brought crowds of strangers together
and taught us to live as faith-filled friends;
Lyman Coleman *who taught me most everything I know*
about creating Village Groups;
Blair Salmons *(my son-in-law) who challenged me*
to write this volume.

Don•Q•Dox: a resource-creation label of The Orlando Fellowship—
an incarnational, missional-ministry community.
Don•Q—The fictional knight *Don Quixote* (Miguel de Cervantes, 1605),
whose most famous adventure includes meeting the tavern prosti-
tute Aldonza and calling her to become the beautiful Dulcinea.
•Dox—Documents/tools/vehicles for discovery.

As the name implies, we are on a quest to discover life as it was meant
to be and invite others to join that quest. We believe that God's image is
planted deeply within each of us, but most times we cannot hear the call
of the "impossible dream" without the company of others who can see in
us things we don't see in ourselves.

THANKS...

To **Lyman Coleman**, who has mentored me for too many years to count—from sleeping next to his first small-group book draft in a retired coal bin to today's encouragement to continue "frog-kissing."

To my **many students** at **Asbury Theological Seminary—Florida Dunnam Campus**, who have shared their wisdom while living through Village Groups each semester.

To **Carolyn Smith**, who reads everything I write, offers corrections with her professional eye, and designs my final work into a book format. This book is evidence of her great work.

The END of Small Groups

CONTENTS

PREFACE - THE DON'S QUEST

As Don Quixote battled windmills across the plains of LaMancha, the Spanish Inquisition was in full burn.[1]

Don Q, the fictional knight (and a symbol of Jesus), created by Miguel de Cervantes (1605), spoke light into those dark days of the Christian Church where death faced those who were declared unorthodox to the faith.

In the classic movie version of his most famous adventure, as Don Quixote battled the evil of his day, he happened upon a wayside tavern. There in the semi-darkness he discovered the barmaid-prostitute Aldonza.[2]

Smitten by love, he declared her his fair lady—Dulcinea. And we all know that an adventurous knight must have a fair lady for whom to dedicate his quests.

Of course, she immediately rejected both him and the dream he attempted to paint into her life. But Don Q never faltered in the face of her rejection.

On each quest, throughout the extended adventure, he carried the "beautiful Dulcinea" on his lips and in his heart. Repeatedly he cast the dream that she's so much more than she sees herself to be. He woos her to a greatness and beauty she cannot imagine.

Though thought a crazy fool, Don never gave up his calling—his mission. To the very end of his life, as Don Quixote's health

---

1 If you're not familiar with this classic, you must watch the ancient movie *Man of LaMancha*, featuring Peter O'Toole, Sophia Loren, James Coco, Harry Andrews, John Castle. DVD release 2004.

2 In Cervantes' original manuscript Don Quixote never actually meets Aldonza. Instead, she is a village girl whom he calls to from a distance, much like Jesus never humanly saw the fulfillment of his calling the Church into being.

began to fail, unconditional love won the day.

And in the midst of her grief and struggle to believe, Aldonza catches a glimpse of her deeper self—the self she had never permitted out of its cage—the self she was created to be.

Then, in a single burst of transformation, she exclaims, "I'm Dulcinea."

EVERYONE'S QUEST

Each human is on a Dulcinea quest to true humanness. A quest to release that image of God planted deep within. Yet most times we cannot hear the call of the "impossible dream" without a company of others—those who can see in us things we cannot see in ourselves.

As leaders, we are offered the amazing privilege of declaring to every Aldonza, "You are Dulcinea."

Of joining with a group of co-adventurers who call forth that creation-self in one another.

NO NEW PROGRAM

Though they may never say it aloud, leaders are often looking for a silver-bullet small group model. They're seeking the latest, trendy program—the one that "really works"—to rejuvenate a dying ministry.

This book isn't about a new program.

Instead, this book is designed as a practical guide for leaders (and potential leaders) of small group communities (Village Groups).[3] It's also for leaders who want to coach other leaders, to begin a multiple small group ministry.

To get to the target, we'll tap into the Bible and other resources. Then I'll give specific, practical guidelines for leading and growing healthy communities of disciples of Jesus. And of course, that's our mission—direct from Jesus those many centuries ago.

If you've read some of the same authors I have, you've noticed

---

3 From this point forward I'll usually refer to any form of small group as a Village Group. Further explanation is coming.

that they believe the whole small group movement began with them. That's just arrogant. And it would be plain dumb for me to pretend I started the resurgence of small groups or that I carry all the answers to group life. However, I will share ideas from my years of observing, leading, and coaching small group ministries.

My most important ministry gift is not in creating new ideas. Rather it's finding ways to apply what others have discovered.

In other words, I'm a practitioner, and that's what you'll find in these pages—practical application. It's reporting what actually works in real life, if followed intentionally.

DON'T READ THIS ALONE!

You may be tempted to read this book alone, to prepare yourself for leading a Village Group. Avoid that temptation.

First, pray and ask God's Spirit to direct you and this vital ministry. God is more concerned that your community group comes to life than you are. So, count on God to guide you, as you give yourself to the Holy Spirit's leading.

Next, the best way to study this book is to practice with others while you learn. You don't want to study ideas that you'll try sometime, once your group gets started. Start with a group from the very beginning.

In other words, recruit a small group of others who are also moving into leadership, or are already leading community groups.

THINK TURBO GROUP

Turbo Groups are a few people, like you, who commit to meet together, and then launch several small group communities all at once. And you won't need a long time to get started. You only need a few weeks to read this book, practice together, then start.

HOW IT WORKS

Plan to meet for six or seven weeks, about two hours each week, as a Turbo Group.

Each week you'll read through one chapter individually, and discuss it at the Turbo Group meeting. At that same weekly meeting you'll work together through the Village Group guide, at the end of each chapter. Take turns leading the Village Group session so each person gets some leading experience, and all will get the flavor of how these groups work.

When you've completed the six weeks' of training, you're ready to start your groups. At this point, there are at least two options for how to get rolling.

1. You can pair up as leaders, serving as co-leaders in a new group; or one will be the leader and the other the apprentice. This should only continue for a short time.[4]
2. An even better idea is for each trained leader to recruit an apprentice who was not in the Turbo Group. Then the two (leader and apprentice) recruit a few group members to get started. The trained leader will train the apprentice on the job using this book as the training tool.

The key to starting is getting started. Don't wait until you think you've learned everything. That time never arrives. You only need to know the basics. You'll learn so much more after your group is going and you make a few mistakes or struggle for answers.

So, relax! Let the adventurous quest of life in a village community begin!

Daryl L. Smith, Winter 2015

---

4 If two trained leaders join together to lead a single group, they each need to quickly look for an apprentice to train and mentor so the one group can soon birth into two groups. We'll discuss this whole birthing process later.

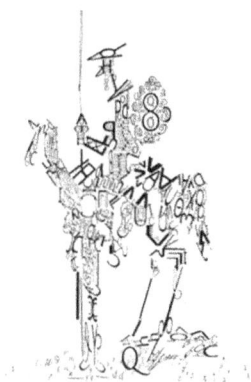

THOUGHT PROVOKERS (for individual reflection):

1. What color comes to mind when you think of small groups—Village Groups? Why do you think your brain chose that color?
2. If you had written this book, what is the most important question you would want answered about leading a Village Group?

TURBO GROUP:

- Work through **Village Group #1** (next page) before going on in your reading.
- You will find a section called **WE SERVE (Our Mission)**. The importance of serving on mission will be explained further on. However, you can start now by choosing a way that you will serve someone this week. Declare your intentions to the group. You will report the results back to the Turbo Group at your next meeting.
- Let the group leader (the one who answers the questions first, guides the group through the questions, and keeps the group on time) be the group member who used an outhouse last. [They must have an adventurous spirit.]

Village Group #1

GATHERING:

1. On a scale of 1 (give up easily) to 10 (pig-headed), how would your family rate your persistence level?

FINDING OUR STORIES IN THE STORY:

Luke 15:11–32 (MSG)

[11-12] Then he said, "There was once a man who had two sons. The younger said to his father, 'Father, I want right now what's coming to me.'
[12-16] "So the father divided the property between them. It wasn't long before the younger son packed his bags and left for a distant country. There, undisciplined and dissipated, he wasted everything he had. After he had gone through all his money, there was a bad famine all through that country and he began to hurt. He signed on with a citizen there who assigned him to his fields to slop the pigs. He was so hungry he would have eaten the corncobs in the pig slop, but no one would give him any.
[17-20] "That brought him to his senses. He said, 'All those farmhands working for my father sit down to three meals a day, and here I am starving to death. I'm going back to my father. I'll say to him, Father, I've sinned against God, I've sinned before you; I don't deserve to be called your son. Take me on as a hired hand.' He got right up and went home to his father.
[20-21] "When he was still a long way off, his father saw him. His heart pounding, he ran out, embraced him, and kissed him. The son started his speech: 'Father, I've sinned against God, I've sinned before you; I don't deserve to be called your son ever again.'
[22-24] "But the father wasn't listening. He was calling to the servants, 'Quick. Bring a clean set of clothes and dress him. Put the family ring on his finger and sandals on his feet. Then get a grain-fed heifer and roast it. We're going to feast! We're going to have a wonderful time! My son is here—given up for dead and now alive! Given up for lost and now found!' And they began to have a wonderful time.
[25-27] "All this time his older son was out in the field. When the day's work was done he came in. As he approached the house, he heard the music and dancing. Calling over one of the houseboys, he asked what was going on. He told him, 'Your brother came home. Your father has ordered a feast—barbecued beef!—because he has him home safe and sound.'
[28-30] "The older brother stalked off in an angry sulk and refused to join in. His father came out and tried to talk to him, but he wouldn't listen. The son said, 'Look how many years I've stayed here serving you, never giving you one moment of grief, but have you ever thrown a party for me and my friends? Then this son of yours who has thrown away your money on whores shows up and you go all out with a feast!'
[31-32] "His father said, 'Son, you don't understand. You're with me all the time, and

everything that is mine is yours—but this is a wonderful time, and we had to celebrate. This brother of yours was dead, and he's alive! He was lost, and he's found!'"

2. At which point in the story do you identify with the father? At that point, which word would most describe your response to your sons? Why?
    a. Grief—for my sin and both my sons' sin
    b. Forgiveness—truly unconditional
    c. Generosity—let's have a party for all
    d. Other _____

3. Suppose that Jesus meant for the father to represent God. What is the good word you need to hear from this story?

ACCOUNTABILITY and CARING:

4. If you were to become a spiritual "father" or "mother" in the image of God shown in this story, how would your life need to change?

5. What is the next step you need to take to become that spiritual parent God is calling you to become?

6. How can this group help you this week to take the next step?
    a. Call you on Monday
    b. Send you an email every other day
    c. Pray for you
    d. Other _____

WE SERVE (OUR MISSION):

(What mission do you intend to complete this week?)

_____

_____

_____

_____

_____

WE PRAY:

Pray silently for one another around your circle. The leader close by praying out loud.

FROM THE CLASSICS

"A human being is nothing but a story with skin around it."
—**Fred Allen** (1894–1956; radio and TV comedian, actor)

CHAPTER 1 - MULTIPLE LENSES

We each carry our own perspectives into any discussion—lenses through which we view, evaluate, and decide.

To help you understand MY perspectives, and the meaning of some of my terms, let me describe a few of my lenses. I trust this self-disclosure gives fuller context to the remainder of the book.

Since everything is about story, I trust that our stories will connect somewhere along this journey and you will know when it happens.

ONE—To know my story, you must know that small or Village Groups define the key facets of my life and ministry. That's why you'll sense my personal passion flooding these pages.

TWO—I rarely use the term *small groups*. It raises concerns for too many people. And it's not profound enough to describe what should be happening when a group connects together inwardly—and outwardly in ministry to their neighbors and the world.

Most Christians I meet react skeptically to the idea of small groups. Some small groups have bored people to death. Others have left emotionally damaged people.

If you came to adulthood in the 1960s and 70s like I did, some small groups took on rare forms. One group, for example, gathered naked people in a swimming pool. There they held hands, and hummed—seeking spiritual insight. Those groups never really caught on in the church nor helped the small group movement's reputation—except possibly with those in the pool.

I prefer a different term—*Village Group*—because it carries such powerful imagery. Ideally, villages are places where

... everyone belongs,

... people are safe to be themselves,

... everyone is equipped for ministry,

... each one is cared for,

... there is a common purpose or mission, and

... you can always come home.

As the ancient proverb says, "It takes a village to raise a child." It also takes a village to grow a disciple of Jesus.

I also use the term *community groups*.

THREE—the word *Church* describes the world-wide group of people who claim to follow Jesus. I also know that *church* is popularly used to describe the facility where the *Church* gathers. I will attempt to refer to *Church* only when it describes the group of Jesus-following people.

FOUR—I try to avoid labels. Terms like conservative or liberal have become tarnished, and identified with specific USAmerican political parties.

However, if I self-labeled, I'd choose *radical*.

I like the taste of *radical* on my tongue!

To capture the root-form for *radical* think radish or carrot—rooted. On some issues, radicals may appear conservative—on others, liberal. It's hard to keep *radicals* in a *proper* box.

Jesus was a radical, rooted in God's kingdom—so radical that those conservative Pharisees and liberal zealots banded together to kill him. I try to identify with his Kingdom-of-God radicalness, and live accordingly.

BUT IS RADICAL TOO HARD?

I've just finished coaching a congregational ministry. After several months of working together, they decided not to pay the price. They launched a new congregation the "old fashioned way"; focusing on attracting a crowd to the weekend, one-hour event they call worship.

All the hours we worked together, to discover how to create communities of people who grow together, grow more like Jesus, and serve their world—went out the window.

It's always harder to create healthy communities than to grow *nickels and noses.*[1]

Please READ THAT LINE AGAIN.

This congregation short-circuited their long-term future for short-term results in order to keep their denomination's financial support and approval on the annual report.

Unfortunately I donated my time.

I've discovered that most groups like *free*; they just don't care so much for *change*. And becoming 21st-century disciples will take a *radical shift* in how we do "church"—similar to what the Jewish Early Church struggled to do 2,000 years ago.

CHRISTENDOM IS OUT!

In case you've not yet noticed…let me be the first to tell you. Just as we're discovering the reality of global climate-change, spiritual climate-change has already happened. The Christian church world has shifted.

Christendom[2] is dead!

It actually died long ago. We're just waking to that reality in the United States.

---

1 This thought was first introduced to me when reading *The Present Future* (San Francisco: Jossey-Bass, 2003) by Reggie McNeal. If you're not familiar with him, you need to digest everything he's written.

2 In my simplistic terms, *Christendom* is the period of history we've been living through since Constantine (272-337AD) was the Roman Emperor. He essentially merged the church and government. And that became the model for the Western world. In USAmerica the church-state merger has been the reality for much of our history (especially for Protestants), despite claims by our forebears from Europe that they came to this continent to escape church-state oppression.

Yet most USAmerican[3] congregations and denominations continue to pretend the world is the same. If we just keep doing the same old things, yet do them harder, and advertise better, we can bring back the "good ole days."

Unfortunately, the "good ole days" only demonstrate our amnesia, not reality.

That leaves us with a couple of choices.

First, in USAmerica, we can keep trying to control peoples' behavior by fighting for political power, and pretending that Christians are the majority culture.

If we choose that struggle, attempting to wrestle political control from those we don't agree with, we'll eventually fizzle off into nothingness. Although, since such big money stands behind the political controllers, the fizzle may take an *eternity* in coming and the kingdom of God will be thwarted in the process.

A better choice would be to celebrate our freedom from the blending of faith and culture—a perverted form of Christianity— and live out God's kingdom life in all its abundance and vitality. That is the world-view that Jesus and the 1st-century church landed in. And anyone who knows the story would call their mission successful.

So, when we step up to the challenge of living and ministering incarnationally in the post-Christendom freedom, God will use us to help bring God's kingdom on earth much like it is in heaven. And haven't we prayed for that, for centuries?

DISCIPLESHIP IS IN!

Actually, ever since Jesus gave the first instructions to his early followers clinging to that mountainside, ***discipleship is the mission.***

---

3   When referring to my country of origin, I usually say USAmerica. Author, futurist, and all-around prophet Leonard Sweet was the first I saw use the term. My colleagues have also challenged me to never call myself an *American*. As nationals from South, Central, and North America, they are also *Americans*, just like I am. So I differentiate between my country of origin and other American countries with *USAmerica*.

Yet, we continue to pour tons of money and energy into great programs and see few disciples of Jesus.

We've mistakenly thought that discipleship begins when a person cleans themself up enough to look like us, declares faith in Jesus, and comes inside the walls of our ministry center. We've forgotten the archaic term *prevenient grace*—God already at work before we arrive.

DISCIPLESHIP = God's missional plan

VILLAGE GROUP = God's primary tool to accomplish the mission

The truth is, the human part of *discipleship* begins the first time a non-believing person encounters a believer who demonstrates Jesus. It continues until a person becomes a fully-devoted follower of Jesus. And yes, that's a growing, life-long process. So, in truth, discipleship (and discipling) never ends.

To be clear, we've often substituted what we call Christian Education for discipleship. Our CE programs fill people's heads with content but rarely help them grow in healthy relationships with one another and with God.[4]

In other words, *cognition has replaced healthy relationships*.

Throughout this book, I'm working from the assumption that *discipleship* (becoming a disciple of Jesus) is the underlying foundation for all our discussion—it is our **mission**.

And a Village Group is God's **primary tool** for growing us as those disciples of Jesus—to accomplish the discipleship mission.

---

4 Before you give up on me, let me say I'm a trained Christian Educator, have been a Christian Education pastor for many years, and have a degree in Instructional Design Systems. In other words, I'm talking about myself—because I write CE curriculum. From my experience, most times we've limited Christian Education to educating brains rather than total transformation of a person.

IT MAY GET YOU FIRED

However, let me caution you!

If you attempt to live what you're reading in these pages, your ministry will be radically changed. If you're a pastor, your congregation may try to get rid of you. If you're a ministry staff member, you may get fired by your senior pastor. Both have happened to me.

As I've mentioned, when coaching churches I find most are not willing to make the radical shift to become truly alive to God's kingdom work. It's too painful for people who've lived in the rut for way too long.

If you're not a paid church staff person—simply a radical person seeking to help change the world—you have a special opportunity. You may get to actually see it happen. And you'll be part of the change.

IT'S ALL ABOUT STORY—Three Stories

We each live our own stories.

Life is all about story. That's why movies and drama grab our hearts so deeply.

To capture the essence of discipleship and life in Village Groups, we must connect our stories.

We were created to join THREE stories: God's story, your story, my story.

God's story runs since before time and continues forever into the future. The story continually calls us back home, even when we don't hear it.

The Bible is God's primary storyteller.

But we must not let arrogance short-circuit God's story from our lives. We each come to Scripture with our own multi-layered lenses of understanding.[5] To get the fullest biblical understanding, we must always filter our interpretation through the lenses of

---

5 Sound familiar? We must never say, "I just read the Bible." No one is wise enough to understand the Bible completely and correctly on their own. Even the apostles had disagreements (check out Acts 15:28, "It seemed good to the Holy Spirit...") over various Scripture passages. We cannot do better. We can only work together for the best understanding we can get.

DISCIPLESHIP = God's missional plan

VILLAGE GROUP = God's primary tool to accomplish the mission

THREE STORIES = God's relational design for the mission

• *faith-traditions* (what we've learned from our parents of faith),

    • *reason* (what we understand through brain power, study, creation, science), and

        • *experience* (what we've learned from life).

All within the context of a *believing community*.

Your story is what you've been living since birth.

The same is true for *my story*.

When these stories travel separately from one another, we remain strangers to one another and God. When the three stories intersect, we become friends.

Jesus said that when two or three *or four* (author's addition) people come together in his name, he shows up.[6]

WRESTLER RON

Meet my friend, Wrestler Ron.

Wrestler Ron was thirteen years old when he striped his hair orange and began adding piercings across his body. He was laughed at and scorned out of the church he attended.

Because the congregational people looked beyond his amazingly creative gifts to the outward body trappings, he was viewed as a potential troublemaker, no matter that he'd never acted out.

6 Author's translation of Matthew 18:20.

Over the years Wrestler Ron survived on his athletic and acting ability with the IWG.[7]

He's now 34 years old, married and has a new baby girl. Something inside tells him that his daughter—and he and his wife—need a focus beyond themselves. Maybe something spiritual that would give deeper meaning to the performance stage they've lived on for so long. A place his daughter would be safe. A group of people who would never think of judging, but would accept them as they are—questions, doubts, beer, curse words and all.

Where can he turn?

Is your or my ministry center a safe place for him to look at faith again?

Probably not, if the truth be told!

Does he have a neighbor who attends a safe Village Group? We can hope…

or we can be intentional to make sure it happens.

THOUGHT PROVOKERS (for individual reflection):

1. What comes to your mind when you think of a Village?
2. What are TWO potential difficulties and THREE advantages of living in a Village?
3. Who in your neighborhood is most like Wrestler Ron? How might you begin to build a relationship with him or her?

TURBO GROUP:

• Work through **Village Group #2.**
• Let the group leader be the person who drove the furthest to get to your gathering, as long as it's not the same person who led last time (in which case, use the person who comes in second for distance. [These are the persistent people.]
• After you've reported in from your last mission (from **WE SERVE**), declare a new mission to complete before the next group meeting.

7 International Wrestling Group—a pseudonym.

Village Group #2

GATHERING:

1. When were you fired from a job, or told you just weren't good enough to do a job right? Was it because you did something wrong or just a misunderstanding? Can you tell what it was? How did you feel afterward?

FINDING OUR STORIES IN THE STORY

Genesis 39:1–21 (NIV)

[1] Now Joseph had been taken down to Egypt. Potiphar, an Egyptian who was one of Pharaoh's officials, the captain of the guard, bought him from the Ishmaelites who had taken him there.
[2] The Lord was with Joseph so that he prospered, and he lived in the house of his Egyptian master. [3] When his master saw that the Lord was with him and that the Lord gave him success in everything he did, [4] Joseph found favor in his eyes and became his attendant. Potiphar put him in charge of his household, and he entrusted to his care everything he owned. [5] From the time he put him in charge of his household and of all that he owned, the Lord blessed the household of the Egyptian because of Joseph. The blessing of the Lord was on everything Potiphar had, both in the house and in the field. [6] So Potiphar left everything he had in Joseph's care; with Joseph in charge, he did not concern himself with anything except the food he ate.
Now Joseph was well-built and handsome, [7] and after a while his master's wife took notice of Joseph and said, "Come to bed with me!"
[8] But he refused. "With me in charge," he told her, "my master does not concern himself with anything in the house; everything he owns he has entrusted to my care. [9] No one is greater in this house than I am. My master has withheld nothing from me except you, because you are his wife. How then could I do such a wicked thing and sin against God?" [10] And though she spoke to Joseph day after day, he refused to go to bed with her or even be with her.
[11] One day he went into the house to attend to his duties, and none of the household servants was inside. [12] She caught him by his cloak and said, "Come to bed with me!" But he left his cloak in her hand and ran out of the house.
[13] When she saw that he had left his cloak in her hand and had run out of the house, [14] she called her household servants. "Look," she said to them, "this Hebrew has been brought to us to make sport of us! He came in here to sleep with me, but I screamed. [15] When he heard me scream for help, he left his cloak beside me and ran out of the house."
[16] She kept his cloak beside her until his master came home. [17] Then she told him this story: "That Hebrew slave you brought us came to me to make sport of me. [18] But as soon as I screamed for help, he left his cloak beside me and ran out of the house."

[19] When his master heard the story his wife told him, saying, "This is how your slave treated me," he burned with anger. [20] Joseph's master took him and put him in prison, the place where the king's prisoners were confined.
But while Joseph was there in the prison, [21] the Lord was with him; he showed him kindness and granted him favor in the eyes of the prison warden.

2. What do you think was Joseph's greatest asset for survival in Egypt?

3. What do think Joseph's first thoughts were once landing in prison?
   a. hang this God stuff   b. God will care for me
   c. I might as well have gone to bed with her
   d. I need to get out of here   e. other _____

4. Which of Joseph's challenges would be the hardest for you?
   a. isolation from family   b. slavery
   c. sexual harassment   d. prison
   e. other _____

ACCOUNTABILITY and CARING:

5. What part of your life may be the most vulnerable right now, because of the stress or temptation you're struggling with? How can this group help you?

WE SERVE (OUR MISSION):

_____

_____

_____

_____

WE PRAY:

Pray *silently* for the person on your *right*. One person close with verbal prayer.

FROM THE CLASSICS

*Since people don't have the courage to mature
unless someone has faith in them, we have to reach those
we meet at the level where they stopped developing,
where they were given up as hopeless,
and so withdrew into themselves and began to
secrete a protective shell because they thought
they were alone and no one cared.
They have to feel they're loved very deeply
and very boldly
before they dare appear humble and kind,
affectionate, sincere and vulnerable.*[1]

1 From Louis Evely, *That Man in You*, translated by Edmond Bonin (Ramsey, NJ: Paulist Press, 1964). Copyright by the Missionary Society of St. Paul the Apostle in the State of New York.

CHAPTER 2 - MY STORY

CHALLENGED

I first heard of small groups as a new college freshman. Obviously, they'd been around for thousands of years, in one form or another. But they were never part of my experience.

During my first week on campus, Al Turner, a fifth-year senior (and mentor), cornered me and offered two pieces of advice. Though not a direct quote, it went something like:

"First, now you're an adult so buy a Day-Timer and start keeping a schedule." (I've continued that practice in the subsequent decades; now in Apple iPad form.)

"Second, we're starting a new group, actually a set of small groups, to discover what it's like to follow Jesus seriously. You need to be there." (I went, obediently.)

Those weekly gatherings in the corner of the dining hall formed us into a pretty heady group. Al facilitated most of our meetings. Along the way he introduced us to what, we found out later, were some really *important* people.

He took us to *Faith at Work*[1] conferences where we both participated and led groups. We rubbed shoulders with people

1 *Faith at Work* (now renamed Lumunos; check out www.lumunos.org) was a group of Christians, mostly from mainline churches, looking for a vital Christian faith, lacking in their congregations. They gathered periodically for conferences, usually in some hotel ballroom. The conference focus was on teaching and small groups sharing life together around the Bible, for two or three days in a row. Transformation from those conferences was so powerful than most of the people went back to their denominations and transformation happened there as well.

like Bruce Larson, Keith Miller, Lloyd Ogilvie, Heidi Frost, Roberta Hestenes, and Lyman Coleman—all in the prime of their minis-tries—whom we'd never heard of before.

We just knew we should be impressed. We later discovered why.

THE SMALL GROUPS

The small groups were safe places to share our real-life experi-ences in the context of Bible study and profound relationships. This was not Bible study like I'd grown to know in my church. We did no races to see who could find a specific Bible passage the quickest. Instead, we discovered a deeper life in community with one another and with Jesus—a place to belong.

My first semester of college was so transformational[2] that when I went home for Thanksgiving break I declared to my par-ents that I no longer needed to follow the rules I'd been taught. I could now live in love with people and Jesus, and trust God's Spirit to guide me. Understandably, with all that was occurring in the late 1960s, my father imagined his *good boy* had gone off to that liberal college and was now trashing his life in *free love*—along with a few thousand dollars of tuition.

My mother, more patient in her understanding, became a stabilizing force, giving me space to continue growing.

And I did by leaps and bounds.

For the first time, Christian faith was focused on following Jesus instead of keeping a list of rules. Following Jesus was not a solo event. Instead, it was life in a community of like-minded Jesus followers.

A NEW PATH

To say that the small group experiences were transformative

---

2 You'll soon notice my repeated use of the words *transformational* and com-munity. Both are significant to my personal story and the direction of this book. Hopefully their use will be limited enough to not detract from your participation in this story.

is a dramatic understatement. The group anchored me for facing the military draft and deciding whether I would go to Viet Nam and "kill commies for Christ," as so many of my friends did.

With that small-group foundation, my path diverted 180 degrees from where I'd ended high school.

That path included becoming a Conscientious Objector. As a CO I faced the wrath of friends and family who believed I had lost my Christian faith and become a traitor to my country.

Amazing how all that gets distorted together in USAmerica.

Those early years of small group life set me in a new direction that has guided my life ever since. Years later while working on my doctoral dissertation—researching Cooperative Learning among adults—I found that the same principles applied in educational settings as to growing Jesus-followers. The group-life principles are imbedded in who we are—how we humans are created to our core.

When we live and work together in cooperating communities, there is a different result than when we compete against one another or go it alone.

THIS CAN'T BE CHURCH

As a sophomore, we invited one of those *Faith at Work* conference leaders, Lyman Coleman, to lead what the college called "Spiritual Emphasis Week." Instead of traditional worship services with a five-day preacher, Lyman burst our boxes. Using the context of the 1960's culture, he guided us in a week-long process of creating a dining-hall-sized "Coffee House." By week's end we had decorated, written music, scribbled poems, and gathered the campus together for a worship celebration like I'd never seen before.

Guitars stepped in for the organ. An open-mic replaced the preacher. Drama and art loosed our creativity. Life stories were shared—relationships restored. Artistically we walked together through deep experiences with Jesus.

Nothing like the church I was raised in.

Such vitality, such joy, such authenticity.

In my imagination, that week was much like I envision the first-century womb the Early Church was birthed in.

THE NEW TRAJECTORY

Moving from the college scene, many forces pressed in from different directions. The need for a paying job as a trained music educator, who never wanted to teach music, left me without an obvious career. The justice views I had taken, and publicly proclaimed, cut me off from many who had been my friends.

I suspect that's something like being gay in a homophobic world.

My father once asked, "Is there no justice issue that you won't fight for?"

Add to that a couple of broken serious dating-relationships and you've got a pretty lonely life.

BUT, I can never remember considering changing course on this new vision for ministry—on this new discovery of what life as a Jesus-follower could be.

Charging (sometimes limping) into ministry, I committed to helping people discover authentic community with God and other humans. A discovery that includes waking to the *God dream* planted inside each human—a dream that draws us back home to our creator.

That trajectory has guided me from hanging out in the streets with drug addicts to leading an orchestra in a traditional church, from guiding small groups in a new church plant to teaching at a seminary—and many places in between.

MATURING

Over the years, I've led small groups and trained small group leaders. From those exciting college days has now come a maturity of experience that puts a framework around my initial understanding of how small Village Groups work most effectively.

Some maturing came from study, more from trial-and-error field experience, but most from hanging out around *Serendipity-*

type people like Lyman Coleman.[3]

What Lyman discovered is the best of Inductive Bible Study, because it's study within a community of people committed to sharing life together. He found that focusing on cognitive content (filling our heads with facts) is not effective in either building a community or growing Jesus-followers as disciples.

Sounds familiar, doesn't it?

The simple, yet profound fact is this:

When people come together in authentic community to *walk around inside* the Scriptures together, amazing discoveries happen, deep communities form, the Bible becomes more than an ancient book, and people move out in mission to their neighbors and the world.

DISCOVERING SOCIAL VALUES

Outside my denomination, few youth grew up in the Bible Quizzing movement, like I did.

If you didn't, I won't explain it except to say imagine intense Bible memory, aggressive competition, angry losers, and youth who have no understanding of how to apply what they've spent every waking moment memorizing.[4]

I know this is an (slight) exaggeration, to make the point. I also know numbers of former quizzers (including myself) who would never let their children be quizzers. A portion of one youth group I led had to nearly be quarantined from youth activities because they were so elitist and badly-behaving. But they could win Bible quizzes.

So what's the point of my ranting, you ask?

3 Much of the thinking behind this writing is a result of *Serendipity House*—the resourcing company Lyman Coleman created. Through the materials from *Serendipity* and the seminars that Lyman led, thousands of people were trained in effective small group leadership. When Lyman retired, *Serendipity House* was sold to another publisher and has since been dismantled.

4 To soften my criticism slightly, let me add that some coaches do Bible application with their quizzers. But they are the minority. The competition supersedes any biblical application.

The truth is, we don't learn *social values* by rote memory, competition or sermons.

And every Jesus-value (biblical value) is a *social value.*

Decades ago, Lev Vygotsky[5] discovered that we best learn social values inside a social setting. We must live in community with others to try out the values and learn how to apply them. Values like love, joy, peace, patience, etc.

Many millennia before Vygotsky, back at the creation of time, females and males were formed to live in deep-oneness relationships. Relationships modeled by the Creator after the Creative Trinity. From that time forward humans have lived their best when they've followed that creation design.

When we've gone our independent way, things have always turned out badly.

You may remember some of Jesus' many teachings about how a community is to live. For example, he used the bride-and-groom picture to describe his relationship with his church that will go on into eternity. It is apparent that he intends for us to take the model of community seriously.

In the next chapter we'll turn our entire attention toward life in community,

But for my story this was an amazing turning point.

When I discovered that *the image of God root* in each of us was calling us together, to live and learn in community, everything changed. The way I teach, the way I pastor, the way I lead—absolutely everything is different.

No longer can I add a few small groups as an appendage to an already busy congregational schedule. Groups are about living as we were created to live.

Remember, Village Groups are the basic tool for God's mission through the Church.

5 Vygotsky was a Russian psychologist who lived from1896 to 1937. His theories were not well know until the 1970s.

They are a place of
caring for one another, together.
growing more like Jesus, together.
serving the world, together.

THOUGHT PROVOKERS (for individual reflection):

1. What most aggravates you about the author's story? Why do you think it does?
2. Even if the time periods are different, what part of Daryl's story most connects to yours?
3. What *social value* can you name that you heard about while growing up, but it took a *community experience* to help you understand its deeper meaning?

TURBO GROUP:

- Work through **Village Group #3**.
- Let the group leader be the person who has never had a driving ticket. If no one qualifies, then pick someone who's not led before. Make sure to rotate leadership, so everyone is a leader before anyone leads a second time.
- Remember the **WE SERVE**. Make sure to report in and declare a new mission each week.

Village Group #3

GATHERING:

1. Think back to a dreaded family gathering that turned out to be a blessing. What turned out to be the best part?

FINDING OUR STORY IN THE STORY:

Genesis 33:1–17 (MSG)

[1-4] Jacob looked up and saw Esau coming with his four hundred men. He divided the children between Leah and Rachel and the two maidservants. He put the maidservants out in front, Leah and her children next, and Rachel and Joseph last. He led the way and, as he approached his brother, bowed seven times, honoring his brother. But Esau ran up and embraced him, held him tight and kissed him. And they both wept.

[5] Then Esau looked around and saw the women and children: "And who are these with you?" Jacob said, "The children that God saw fit to bless me with."

[6-7] Then the maidservants came up with their children and bowed; then Leah and her children, also bowing; and finally, Joseph and Rachel came up and bowed to Esau.

[8] Esau then asked, "And what was the meaning of all those herds that I met?" "I was hoping that they would pave the way for my master to welcome me."

[9] Esau said, "Oh, brother. I have plenty of everything—keep what is yours for yourself."

[10-11] Jacob said, "Please. If you can find it in your heart to welcome me, accept these gifts. When I saw your face, it was as the face of God smiling on me. Accept the gifts I have brought for you. God has been good to me and I have more than enough." Jacob urged the gifts on him and Esau accepted.

[12] Then Esau said, "Let's start out on our way; I'll take the lead." [13-14] But Jacob said, "My master can see that the children are frail. And the flocks and herds are nursing, making for slow going. If I push them too hard, even for a day, I'd lose them all. So, master, you go on ahead of your servant, while I take it easy at the pace of my flocks and children. I'll catch up with you in Seir."

[15] Esau said, "Let me at least lend you some of my men." "There's no need," said Jacob. "Your generous welcome is all I need or want."

[16] So Esau set out that day and made his way back to Seir. [17] And Jacob left for Succoth. He built a shelter for himself and sheds for his livestock. That's how the place came to be called Succoth (Sheds).

2. What surprises you about Esau's attitude? Why?
   a. he didn't kill Jacob
   b. willingness to protect Jacob
   c. he refused the gifts
   d. other _____

3. What comes to your mind as you think about the next holiday with the extended family?
   a. It's so good
   b. I wish I didn't have to go!
   c. Can hardly wait for the cookin'
   d) other _____

ACCOUNTABILITY and CARING:

4. What's the hardest part of going home for you? Has it gotten better or worse over the years?

5. What have you found that holds you back from mending strained relationships?
   a. I'm ready, they're not
   b. it's too late
   c. timing isn't right
   d. it's too painful
   d. other _____

6. How can this group help you move toward healthier relationships?

WE SERVE (OUR MISSION)

_____
_____
_____
_____
_____

WE PRAY:

Two or three team members pray for the group.

IN THE NEWS

"The notions of self-reliance, self-sufficiency,
which are so strong in the American culture, sort of lead you
to say that if you have problems you should take yourself
by the bootstraps and start working on it."[1]

---

1 Eldar Shafir, William Stewart Tod Professor of Psychology and Public Af-
fairs, Princeton University; https://psych.princeton.edu/~psych/psychology/
research/shafir/index.php; from an National Public Radio article: "For Many
Americans, Stress Takes A Toll on Health and Family" by Richard Knox and
Patti Neighmond, Morning Edition, July 7, 2014. [http://www.npr.org/blogs/
health/2014/07/07/323351759/for-many-americans-stress-takes-a-toll-on-health-
and-family]

CHAPTER 3 - OLD WINE, NEW BOTTLES

INDIVIDUALISM—THE PRIZED VALUE

From the old West cowgirl, with six-shooters on her hips, to contemporary politicians who declare that they pulled themselves up by their own *bootstraps*, individualism hangs deep in our national DNA.

Certainly, we've all heard the stories of underdog teams who've won a great victory. But it's usually the lone hero who gets the award.

What we're discovering is that this macho image is not naturally a USAmerican value as much as it's a male value; mostly an Anglo male value. And since Anglo males have dominated the culture for generations, this individualistic mindset has been propagated on the entire USAmerican culture.

In reality, women of all ethnic backgrounds and most males and females of color are socially communal. The truth be told, most males are uncomfortable with the individualism espoused by much of the USAmerican culture. They're compelled by cultural *pressure* to demonstrate their individualistic prowess. They posture larger than life with big trucks, big guns, and vulgar language.

All to cover their deep sense of inadequacy and sexual vulnerability.

For too many years our most prominent human-developmental researchers were Anglo men, who primarily researched among

Anglo males. Their research espoused *individuation* as the high-est level of human maturity.[1] They then applied their misguided results to all people groups.

Gladly, we're discovering that they were wrong.

Aside from the arrogance of pretending we can go through life on our own, the difficulty of living out this bootstrap mindset is showing up in extreme levels of stress. A recent story on National Public Radio discussed how this individualist thinking is damaging both families and individuals. As individuals try to carry the weight of their stress alone, they can find no relief.[2] People don't seek help when they need it because they might appear weak—not in control. In addition, they have no community to ask for support, nor would they dare. The results show up in violence, broken relationships, health issues, etc.

CREATED FOR COMMUNITY

Being created for community, doesn't mean some "huddle and cuddle"[3] little group.

Modeled after its Trinitarian self, the Holy Trinity (the original Village Group) created the first woman and man to demonstrate a community of oneness that lives and grows vitally within the bounds of time. It culminates in the eternal wedding party of the Church—the Bride—and Jesus—the groom.

This is to be a community formed to grow its members more and more into the image of Jesus, to care for the members' needs, to serve in God's mission to the world.

---

1   See prominent research by Jean Piaget and Lawrence Kohlberg. Two classic sources for discussing these issues are *Moral Development Foundations* by Donald M. Joy (Abingdon, 1983) and *In a Different Voice* by Maggie Scarf (Harvard University Press, 1998). Much additional research has been done in recent years.
2   National Public Radio article: "For Many Americans, Stress Takes A Toll on Health and Family" by Richard Knox and Patti Neighmond, Morning Edition, July 7, 2014.
     [http://www.npr.org/blogs/health/2014/07/07/323351759/for-many-americans-stress-takes-a-toll-on-health-and-family]
3   Alan Hirsch, *The Forgotten Ways* (Grand Rapids: Brazos Press, 2006). p. 221.

Pastor Hank Fortener describes this community life as "a dynamic interdependence between one another and God." In fact Jesus uses the analogy of grapes, not carrots, for this kind of community.[4] Carrots grow completely independent of one another. They live or die on their own. On the other hand, grapes are connected to a vine. They receive nourishment and support together, from the primary vine.

Grapes cannot live without the vine connection.

THE MISSIONAL TASK

Remember, God's over-arching purpose for community is discipleship. We are called to lives as disciples (followers) of Jesus who help grow others as disciples of Jesus, who in turn help grow others as disciples of Jesus.

In an age of social media, most of us have more *friends* than we can count. Yet, research studies show that we are a most lonely people. Social media can never fill our longing void for deep face-to-face relationships.

If deep relationships already exist, then the social media format will help us stay connected. But it can never replace what happens when two or more people share the same space and experience the body language of presence.

As I said above, growing relationships is not just about us feeling cozy. It's about us helping one another grow more like Jesus, so we can better serve the world. That's being a disciple of Jesus. C.S. Lewis got it right when he declared, "If the Church is not doing this, then all the cathedrals, clergy, missions, sermons, even the Bible, are a waste of time."[5]

Alan Hirsch says it this way, "…This [discipleship] is the very task into which Jesus focused his efforts and invested most of his

4   Pastor Hank Fortener, in a sermon preached January 19, 2014 (John 15:1–17) at Mosaic Church, Hollywood, CA. Check out: https://mobile.twitter.com/HankFortener

5   W. Vaus, *Mere Theology: A Guide to the Thought of C.S. Lewis* (Downers Grove, IL: InterVarsity, 2004), p. 167. In Alan Hirsch's, *The Forgotten Ways* (Grand Rapids: Brazos Press, 2006), p. 102.

time and energy, namely in the selection and development of that motley band of followers on whose trembling shoulders he lays the entire redemptive movement that would emerge from his death and resurrection."[6]

PUBLIC GOD

As the creator of community, Jesus knew the secret of living in community. And he modeled it when equipping his disciples for the mission he called them to.

Yet, as we look around our cultural context, maybe the greatest threat to Christian discipleship in USAmerican culture is *consumerism*.[7] And consumerism threatens both those inside and outside the Church.

Instead of describing the value and workings of a product, advertisers appeal to our human worth and spiritual values.

Words like *joy, freedom,* and *happiness* define anything from our soft drinks to our vehicles.

Too often we shop when we are seeking fulfillment, value, and significance. We find comfort and security in the products we purchase.

Products become our individual false god after whose image we are being formed.

Yet as Jesus' disciples we are called to something deeper, more risky, and only discovered in a community of like-minded people.

COMMUNITAS HAPPENS

Hirsch defines this radical *something* by calling us to a more accurate biblical model of community.

He calls it *communitas*.[8]

Communitas goes well beyond "huddle and cuddle" groups.

---

6   Hirsch, *The Forgotten Ways,* p. 102.
7   For a thorough discussion of the issues related to *consumerism*, see Hirsch, *The Forgotten Ways,* particularly page 106 ff.
8   Hirsch, *The Forgotten Ways,* p. 217 ff.

It's a community modeled after Jesus' relationship with his 12 closest followers. It's a community formed by the human need for adventure, for the journey. Most importantly it's a community growing out of the ups and downs of life, bound together by a common mission. A mission too great to fulfill individually.

"[*Communitas*] involves adventure and movement, and it describes that unique experience of *togetherness* that only really happens among a group of people inspired by the vision of a better world who actually attempt to do something about it....It is here where the safe, middle-class consumerist captivity of the church is so very problematic. And it is here where the adaptive challenge of the twenty-first century could be God's invitation to the church to rediscover itself as a missional *communitas*."[9]

As leaders of Village Groups, our role begins by facilitating the discipleship process as we create a community of people desiring, or at least exploring, what it might mean to be a disciple of Jesus. This leaves the door wide open for non-believers who are looking for life-meaning beyond the superficial—the Wrestler Rons among us. And as we find fulfillment in deep, authentic relationships in the context of the Scriptures (God's story), our consumerism is replaced by deeper, authentic significance. A significance found in the mission of God that we are called to join in, as his followers—disciples—living in *communitas*.

DOING IT NATURALLY

A couple of years back, I attended a conference where Hugh Halter and Matt Smay taught us from their *Tangible Kingdom*[10] ministry model. After 24 hours of study, one attendee asked something like, "Is this just another one of those church-growth plans that

9   Hirsch, *The Forgotten Ways*, p. 221–222.
10 Hugh Halter and Matt Smay have created the *Missio* Network. It's a group of people who are exploring wholistic ministry and new ways of living God's Kingdom on earth. Check out their resources such as *The Tangible Kingdom* (San Francisco: Jossey-Bass, 2008), *AND: The Gathered and Scattered Church* (Grand Rapids: Zondervan, 2010), *Bi-Vo* (Missio Pub., 2014), and *Flesh* (David C. Cook, 2014).

come and go?"

Hugh's response struck me, "No. In fact, I hope that we're not even talking about it in five years, because it's the natural way Church is done, coming out of the first century in the book of Acts."

I believe the *Tangible Kingdom* model may best capture the essence of how a ministering community should look. You can read one of their books to get a more complete picture of their model.

For our purposes, let's limit our discussion to three circles.

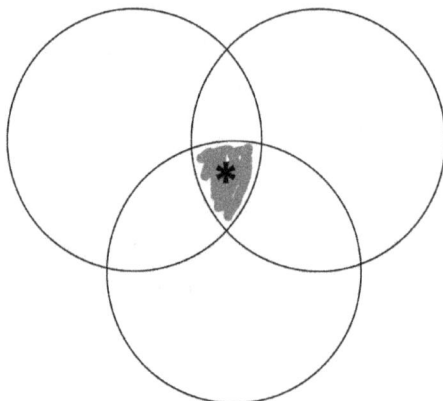

Halter and Smay call one circle, *Communion*. It's what most Christian communities do on a weekend. They gather for worship events, for teaching the adults, children, and youth. Most do this quite well because that's where they mobilize the majority of their volunteers and pastoral staff, and spend most of their money. In fact, if you check your budget, you're probably like most congregations who spend at least 80% of their budget on the weekend.

COMMUNION

It takes lots of money to get sound, lights, smoke, and music just right to attract a 21st-century, entertainment-overdosed crowd.

A second circle is *Inclusive Community*. It's the kind of community we're describing in this book, and what I've called Village Groups. It's where Wrestler Ron can belong from the day he first appears. It's a place where community happens intentionally, because there is a commitment to healthy relationships by all involved. And it's led by a woman or man who is committed to facilitating that healthy community.

COMMUNITY

The expectation of living in an Inclusive Community should be the atmosphere for the entire congregation to breathe; a way of life for every Jesus-follower.

It's where…

… We care for one another's needs.

… We best grow as disciples, because we're doing it together.

… We are equipped to fulfill our ministries.

… We find accountability, to keep us on focus.

… We best serve our neighborhoods and world together

The third intersecting circle is *Mission*. That mission is what the entire congregation targets but fulfills primarily through the Inclusive Community (Village Group) and through each individual who understands that we are all called to mission—to ministry—to serve—with God.

MISSION

When people are growing in deep relationship with one another and with Jesus, and are equipped for the task, they cannot help but step into mission. Staying inside the group walls and serving themselves just doesn't fit with who they are.

This brings us back to *communitas*—a Village Group on God's passionate mission together.

When those three circles *intersect*, the kingdom of God becomes visible (tangible). And that's what every faith community should look like. So instead of focusing all resources on weekend events, those weekend events become wonderful *gathering* celebrations and teaching times, preparing disciples to *scatter*—sharing life in their Inclusive Communities (Village Groups), in service to their neighbors and the world.

EXCUSING OUR BROKENNESS?

I think the worst bumper sticker of all time reads, "Christian Aren't Perfect, Just Forgiven."

You've seen it too.

While it is literally accurate, what it's really implying is, "Since Jesus forgave me for past, present, and future sins with his death on the cross, I can now act any way I want. I don't care who you are, just get out of my way."

In other words, we can flaunt our forgiveness and excuse ourselves when we act like the devil toward other people and creation.

But the unanswered question is this.

Why is there such a gap between what we've just described as the life of Jesus' disciples and *rubber-on-the-road reality*?

For example, from my experience (and probably yours too):

Why am I, as a biker, so often dodging rude and speeding mini-vans with a Jesus-fish on the back?

Why has libertarianism become nearly synonymous with Christian?

Why would a wealthy Christian woman be heartbroken, in sobs, over the fate of the economy, concerned that her kids may not have the same level of income that she has enjoyed?

Why are Christians known mostly for bad news rather than a positive message of Good News, especially on justice issues? Why would any Jesus follower demand gun rights to protect themselves, or try to keep immigrants out of USAmerica, or oppose healthcare for those in need, or oppose those who work to save the environment God gave us to care for?

The short answer is that we're not living as disciples of Jesus.

Jesus' call is for our outside behavior to match our beliefs and words.

Jesus had some strong words to say about how we care for people and his creation, and how he will judge us when he returns.

Instead of growing free from the sin within, we've learned how to manage it better and make excuses for when we don't.

Check out this brief summary where Jesus describes what he's looking for in a disciple's life. (Matthew 25:31–46)

Jesus said we'll be judged on whether

the hungry are fed,
the thirsty are given drink,
the immigrant is protected,
the naked are clothed,
the sick are nursed to health,
the prisoner visited and restored. (author's paraphrase)

That's a bit scary. Then add this list to the rest of Jesus' life and teaching, like the Sermon on the Mount (Matthew 5–7) and we could be terrified about the incongruence between our inner and outer lives.

Yet, rather than terror, our hope is in the fact that Jesus' greatest desire is to recreate both our inner and outer lives.

THE GUTS OF A DISCIPLE

When we peer deeply inside discipleship we discover life-congruency happens when we become people who are transformed from the inside out.

So, let me introduce you to a synonymous term for discipleship: *Spiritual Formation*.

While it's probably not new to you, this term may help us get at the core of what a disciple of Jesus is to look like.

Spiritual Formation is never about completing a list of good things like reading the Bible or praying or following a chart of rules, or even going to a church building whenever the doors are open, as helpful as those things are.

Spiritual formation is the transformation that happens when God's Spirit is working in our character.

It's actually becoming more like Jesus.

In other words, a disciple is a person who is,

In the process of…(a life-long happening)

Being conformed…(taking on a new shape)

To the image of Jesus…(the form who is our pattern)

For the sake of others.[11] (it's never about ourselves)

So, for example, instead of reading the Bible more, to get enough knowledge to manage the sin we wish we didn't commit—tiringly impossible—we ask the Holy Spirit to begin changing our inside lives.

And with the continuing inward change, our outside lives take on a new look as well.

In Galatians 3:19–26, the Apostle Paul describes how this all comes together—letting go of the *old stuff* and letting God's Spirit create new *fruit* in us. He says, "Since we live by the Spirit, let us keep in step with the Spirit." (Galatians 3:25, NIV)

Sounds like a being-set-free dance!

And that *Spiritual Formation*—that "keeping in step with the Spirit," that living as a disciple of Jesus—happens best when we do it together.

Similarly, Anglican priest John Wesley stated long ago that, "Human nature is perfected by participation in groups, not by acting as isolated individuals."[12]

And we do it together best when we have great Village Group leaders to guide us.

---

11 M. Robert Mullholland Jr., *Invitation to a Journey* (Downers Grove, IL: Inter-Varsity, 1993).

12 From John Wesley's Foundational Principles quoted in *John Wesley's Class Meeting: A Model for Making Disciples* by D. Michael Henderson (Nappanee, IN: Evangel Press, 1997), page 128.

THOUGHT PROVOKERS (for individual reflection):

1. Where do you sense the greatest pull toward individualism in your own life?
2. Where is *consumerism* too much of a god in your life…meeting your spiritual or emotional needs?
3. Compare the *Tangible Kingdom* model to the congregational setting where you normally attend.
   How are they similar?
   How are they different?
4. What area of your life needs for you to stop trying to manage it, and to allow God's Holy Spirit to begin recreating it into the image of Jesus? (Where your outside and inside lives don't match up.)

TURBO GROUP:

- Work on **Village Group #4**.
- If your group is large enough, let the group leader be someone who has not led the group previously. Again, make sure to rotate leadership, so everyone leads before anyone leads a second time.

Village Group 4

GATHERING:

1. As an elementary child, what is a time you remember not being chosen for the team? Why do you think you weren't chosen? How long did it take you to get over it?

FINDING OUR STORIES IN THE STORY:

Ephesians 1:1–14 (MSG)

[1] I, Paul, am under God's plan as an apostle, a special agent of Christ Jesus, writing to you faithful Christians in Ephesus. [2] I greet you with the grace and peace poured into our lives by God our Father and our Master, Jesus Christ.
[3] How blessed is God! And what a blessing he is! He's the Father of our Master, Jesus Christ, and takes us to the high places of blessing in him. [4] Long before he laid down earth's foundations, he had us in mind, had settled on us as the focus of his love, to be made whole and holy by his love. [5] Long, long ago he decided to adopt us into his family through Jesus Christ. (What pleasure he took in planning this!) [6] He wanted us to enter into the celebration of his lavish gift-giving by the hand of his beloved Son.
[7] Because of the sacrifice of the Messiah, his blood poured out on the altar of the Cross, we're a free people—free of penalties and punishments chalked up by all our misdeeds. And not just barely free, either. Abundantly free! [8] He thought of everything, provided for everything we could possibly need, [9] letting us in on the plans he took such delight in making. He set it all out before us in Christ, [10] a long-range plan in which everything would be brought together and summed up in him, everything in deepest heaven, everything on planet earth.
[11] It's in Christ that we find out who we are and what we are living for. Long before we first heard of Christ and got our hopes up, he had his eye on us, had designs on us for glorious living, [12] part of the overall purpose he is working out in everything and everyone.
[13] It's in Christ that you, once you heard the truth and believed it (this Message of your salvation), found yourselves home free—signed, sealed, and delivered by the Holy Spirit. [14] This signet from God is the first installment on what's coming, a reminder that we'll get everything God has planned for us, a praising and glorious life.

2. What part of this Bible section most grabs your imagination?
   a. being holy   b. our new family relationship
   c. knowing God's will   d. unity of earth and heaven
   e. other _____
   What color would you use to describe this passage? Why?

3. Re-read vs. 4 and 13–14. How would you explain to a new Jesus-follower about God's desire for us to be holy, and the Holy Spirit's seal on our lives?

As a group, try to write down a simple explanation of this big concept that makes sense to you.

ACCOUNTABILITY and CARING:

4. If Jesus showed up at your door with a megaphone and yelled, "You've been chosen...," what is the most exciting thing he could say to you to complete the sentence?

5. If you really believed, deep down, that you are especially chosen by God, how might that impact your feelings about yourself? Your ministry? Your family?

6. How can the group help you this week?

WE SERVE (OUR MISSION):

_____
_____
_____
_____
_____

WE PRAY:

One or two volunteers pray for the group members and their upcoming missions.

FROM THE CLASSICS

"A Christian small group is an intentional, face-to-face gathering of 3 to 12 people on a regular time schedule with the common purpose of discovering and growing in the possibilities of the abundant life in Christ."—**Roberta Hestenes**

Consider the elements of this definition:

Intentional: Group members choose to covenant together in agreement with the responsibilities and accountability of being a group member.

Face-to-face: Since up to 90% of communication is non-verbal, when people gather face-to-face, honesty, freedom, trust, evaluation, and growth is produced.

3–12 people: With less than three people you don't have a group. With more than 12, you lose intimacy.

Regular time schedule: It is essential for a group to meet weekly at the beginning so bonding occurs. After about six weeks the group can meet less often but must continue meeting consistently to foster loyalty among group members.

Common purpose: The group must have a common purpose and mission for group members to continue growing as disciples of Jesus.

Discovering and growing: A small group is the best place for both non-believers and believers to discover more about following Jesus, and grow more like him.

The abundant life in Christ: Small groups are the best place for people to come together as a community through prayer, Bible study, fellowship, accountability, and service.[1]

---

1 Adapted from *The Serendipity Encyclopedia* by Lyman Coleman (Littleton, CO: Serendipity House, 1997), p. 52.

CHAPTER 4 - CALLING SERVANT LEADERS

The primary point of this book is to equip Village Group leaders.

To build on what we've already discussed, it's time to turn our focus toward leadership and what it looks like from Jesus' point of view. We'll then be prepared to jump into the details of guiding a Village Group.

Of course, any time we mention leadership, someone asks the question, "Are leaders born or taught?" The answer is, "Yes." Some people are born with natural gifts for leading but need help to fine-tune those gifts. Others without the natural gifts can learn the basic skills to become a leader. Yet, everyone is a leader of some sort, leading someone. The difference is whether we are good or poor leaders; whether or not we take responsibility for those we lead.

A SERVANT LEADER?

The leadership model demonstrated by Jesus is Servant Leadership.

Yes, Servant Leadership.

In recent years, businesses have led the way as Servant Leaders—better than most ministries—because they've found that Servant Leaders are the most effective leaders. Servant Leaders nurture the best employees, create satisfied customers, care for their environments and communities, and grow profitable companies.

Plain and simple, Servant Leadership just works.

Yet, the idea of Servant Leadership sounds like an oxymoron. How can a person be both a servant and a leader? Good question. Let me give you a little history.

The term *servant leader* was actually coined by Robert Greenleaf, back in the 1970s when he worked with AT&T, the phone company. Interestingly, he discovered the idea from Jesus. He decided to try it in a business setting and found great success as he and others began to apply the principles of *servant leadership* to their various contexts.

Robert Greenleaf's definition would be a great place for us to start in our ministries. He defined Servant Leadership in terms of consequences on the people being led, as:

"Do those being served grow as persons: do they while being served, become healthier, wiser, freer, more autonomous, more likely themselves to become servants? And what is the effect on the least privileged in society; will she or he benefit, or, at least, not be further deprived....[Making sure that] no one will knowingly be hurt by the action, *directly or indirectly.*"[1]

At first glance, that sounds obviously clear and to the point. But in real time and real space it's not necessarily easy to live out. In fact, Greenleaf believed that "For the...ones among us who are 'in charge,' nothing short of a 'peak' experience, like religious conversion or psychoanalysis or an overpowering new vision, seems to have much chance of converting a confirmed non-servant into an affirmative servant."[2]

In other words, he believed that Servant Leadership was Jesus' way. He believed that Servant Leadership is the very best way to lead whether in business or ministry. But he also believed that we are so ingrained with a desire for power that we cannot become servant leaders without a radical life transformation.

---

1 See *The Power of Servant Leadership by* Robert K. Greenleaf, (San Francisco: Berrett-Koehler, 1998), p. 43.
2 Greenleaf, p. 23.

GOD'S DESIGN

Long before Robert Greenleaf, there was God and God had a plan. And God's plan included humans who are created for deep healthy relationships. And like those relationships demonstrated in Genesis chapter one and two, we are called to live in partnership with one another.

Man and woman in partnership[3], serving each other.

All humans in partnership, in community, serving one another.

We don't know how long it took, but the creation dream seems short-lived for in Genesis 3, the dream was destroyed. The woman and man—seduced by the serpent and willfully defiant—decide to go their own direction, breaking relationship with God and with each other.

The final act of sabotage came in Genesis chapter 3 verse 20.

In a statement of dominion and power over the woman, the man took the name *adam* for himself—stealing the name given to both woman and man together—the name of ultimate dignity and worth. He declared himself Adam and named the woman Eve—"child bearer."

Just as the human had named the animals in Genesis 2, the man took lordship over the woman by naming her. Instead of co-stewardship as God had directed, the man took the authority for himself and demoted the woman to the status of other created beings. And instead of an exalted name, he gave her a functionary one. From that point forward her value would come as the incubator of humanity; one who births and nurses.

From the pinnacle of creation, our fore-parents fell into the

---

3 The Hebrew word *adam* originally was a term for both woman and man together, taken from *adamah* (earth). The image of God was planted in both of them. Before Genesis 3:20 we do not have Adam and Eve—those are terms of the *fall*—sin entering the equation. Previously we had the "first woman" (Hebrew *Ishsha*) and "first man" (Hebrew *Ish*). For a fuller study of this material see *More Than a Great Wedding: creating healthy communities where relationships thrive* (Lulu. com or Amazon.com, 2009).

sin-filled pit. The man and woman broke relationship with God, destroyed their relationship with each other—and sin entered the world. The man took on the authority of God and the woman became an object for use.

And all relationships became a struggle for power.

Mercifully, God didn't abandon the first man and first woman in their brokenness—refusing to let them live forever in their sin. He banished them, away from the "Tree of Life," sending them out from that garden of wonderful beginnings to an uncertain and grief-filled future.

A quick glance through the Old Testament should easily bring us to tears as the story of pain cycles and recycles—from struggles for independence to periods of repentance; from heeding God's loving call to spurning that call. Trapped in their world of might-makes-right, individuals and nations struggled for control over one another.

JESUS THE DEMONSTRATOR

After centuries and centuries of struggle, when the time was just right, Jesus appeared on the earthly scene. And he stirred the pot by denouncing those old systems.

In fact, to the very end of his life, even on the night of his betrayal, Jesus drew the analogy for the faith community. He demonstrated how this life of mutual service should be carried out. He pulled off his cloak, wrapped a towel around his waist, grabbed the water basin, dropped to his knees, and washed his disciples' feet.

He could have given the order for Peter or James or John to do it. Hadn't they just been bickering over who would be the most powerful in Jesus' kingdom? What a great opportunity to put them in their "rightful" place—with the disciples serving the leader.

Yet Jesus didn't do that.

He gave them the lesson of a lifetime. And you can imagine that he had their full attention when he stood up and said, "Listen up, boys. You argue over who is to be the greatest but this is how it's done in God's kingdom. Learn how to be a servant" (author's paraphrase).[4]

From our Western mindsets, with the monarchical influence of presidents, kings, popes and bishops, we have been conditioned to have a verticalized concept of leadership; thus we tend to view the Trinity as a hierarchy. We then wrongly transfer that concept into [all] our...relationships.[5]

From our distorted vantage point, we doubt the real possibility for two humans to truly become one, in the image of God.

And to carry the logic forward, if two can never be one, how can a whole community become one?

Yet, Jesus doesn't let us off the hook. We are still called to live in unity, in healthy community groups.

To know the oneness of the original creation.

GROWING DISCIPLES

The apostle Paul picks up on Jesus' theme in his letter to the Ephesian church. In chapter four he declares:

[11] So Christ himself gave the apostles, the prophets, the evangelists, the pastors and teachers, [12] to equip his people for works of service, so that the body of Christ may be built up [13] until we all reach unity in the faith and in the knowledge of the Son of God and become mature, attaining to the whole measure of the fullness of Christ.

[14] Then we will no longer be infants, tossed back and forth by the waves, and blown here and there by every wind of teaching and by the cunning and craftiness of people in their deceitful scheming.

[15] Instead, speaking the truth in love, we will grow to become in every respect the mature body of him who is the head, that is,

4 See John 13–17. Jesus not only demonstrates the community but also prays that their oneness would so model the Trinity that non-believers couldn't miss the message.

5 Moltmann, Jürgen, *The Trinity and the Kingdom: The Doctrine of God* (Minneapolis: Fortress Press, 1993), p. 19ff. Moltmann lays out this thesis of cultural hierarchicalism "invading" the Western church in chapter 6, "The Kingdom of Freedom."

Christ. ¹⁶ From him the whole body, joined and held together by every supporting ligament, grows and builds itself up in love, as each part does its work. (Ephesians 4:11–16, NIV)

In other words, Paul is saying your role as a leader is to use your God-given gifts to equip—facilitate—mentor your group members into growing to maturity as Jesus-followers. Then as Jesus followers, they use their God-given gifts to do the same with the people in their spheres of influence. That's called discipleship—a disciple of Jesus.

Equipping is never a matter of competing. It's helping everyone cooperate together to come to full maturity. And as we discussed earlier, when we learn together, we learn best.

SERVANT LEADERS DO WHAT?

At this point you're probably asking (I would be if I were you), "How, in practical ways, is a Servant Leader different than other leaders." Or, "What might servant leading look like in my Village Group?"

So, here are some practical applications to get you started.

You will serve in at least two directions at the same time.

If you're not the lead pastor, you'll have to discover how to serve your supervisor. If you are a lead pastor you must answer to a board or overseer. Helping them fulfill their goals and dreams will be important for your future work in ministry. Whoever chose you to lead a Village Group had some specific ideas in mind about what should happen in those groups, and how it should get done.

In addition, you will serve the members of the group you lead.

1. You will look out for their needs as you guide them in their spiritual growth. You will also teach your group members to care for one another—helping them network with resources for meeting those needs.

2. You will help the group make decisions. It may involve when to meet or where to serve. You will guide, but your role of guiding toward the best decisions will not come through coercion or manipulation. Instead, you will be a good persuader. And per-

suasion is not just another word for manipulating; instead it's truly valuing other peoples' viewpoints.

Servant Leaders are not dictators who demand their own way, nor are they totally passive, letting the group do whatever they want. Servant Leaders cast vision for where the groups should be going and how individual members should be growing. They speak the truth wisely and gently, to hold people accountable. At the same time Servant Leaders offer immense grace to those who are struggling.

As a ministry leader, we have no ability to demand that people do anything. If we were paying the group members to attend meetings or serve in the neighborhood, we could stop paying them if they didn't do what we told them to do. That's not possible in a community of Jesus-followers. Group members will follow us because they are committed to God's kingdom or because we helped them catch a bigger picture of a greater future.

3. One of the great evils in USAmerican leadership myths is that we don't need to depend on others—that we can lead alone. To quote one of my dad's favorite statements, "That's hogwash!" (I have no idea what *hogwash* is, but it makes the point.) We are all interdependent with one another, whatever our role in a group.

4. Servant leaders take responsibility or blame, when things go badly. They give away credit to others, never taking it for themselves.[6] As a leader who holds others accountable for their growth as disciples of Jesus, the Servant Leader recognizes they're own need for growth and accepts accountability from the other group members.

5. The Servant Leader models serving in the neighborhood and the world by his or her own service. They don't do the entire ministry. Instead they keep the serving-vision in front of the group, and join in the serving.

---

6 For a thorough look at this kind of Level 5 leadership, check out *Good to Great* by Jim Collins (New York: Harper Collins, 2001) and *Good to Great and the Social Sectors*: a monograph to accompany *Good to Great* by Jim Collins (www.jimcollins.com, 2005) ISBN-978-0-9773264-0-2.

6. A Servant Leader is a **pastor** to their group.

That's right, a *Pastor*.

Try saying that out loud to yourself:

"I am a pastor to this small group of people."

Congratulations, you did it!

You're not just a facilitator of meetings or arranger of service opportunities. You will guide the group and care for the group members' needs.

But before you reject the idea outright, think about it for a minute. Your larger congregational community probably has someone you call "Pastor" (or Reverend, or whatever), who oversees the larger ministry of the congregation. However, you've probably noticed that there is no way for one person to meet a congregation's many needs. The best care comes when a Village Group, led by its leader, takes responsibility for its members. You are the *front-line pastor* to your *congregation*.

In other words, you are modeling the life of a DISCIPLE.

This pastoring model may primarily consist of leading the Village Group sessions. It should also include staying alert to the emotional, spiritual, and physical needs of your group members. It may mean hospital visitation or rallying the group for special support of a team member who is facing a crisis.

BRING IT TOGETHER

As a leader, a Servant Leader of a Village Group (or any leadership role for that matter), you are called to lead your people—by serving—by leading—both at the same time.

In Jesus' model, serving and leading can never be artificially pulled apart. They are two parts of the same whole.

Think about it this way: a coach!

We are all aware of various kinds of sports coaches. Some are better than others.

All work their hardest to win through their team's players.

Some yell and scream—throwing tantrums at the referees.

Some sit calmly on the sidelines, strategizing the next play.
But long before there were sports coaches, there was another kind of coach.

Did you guess it?

It was a carriage that carried special people, the rich, the roy-alty—precious cargo—from one place to another.

Now put those two together.

Our role as a Servant Leader of a Village Group is to *carry* the people in our group (precious cargo) from where they are right now, to where God wants them to be when they leave our sphere of influence.

That's Coaching.

That's Pastoring.

That's Mentoring.

That's Facilitating.

That's Servant Leading.

THOUGHT PROVOKERS (for individual reflection):

1. How would you define Servant Leadership for a popular newspaper in 50 words or less?
2. Which role of servant leading, discussed in this chapter, most captures your imagination—most excites you?
3. What two questions do you have about leading that you still need answers for?

TURBO GROUP:

- Work on **Village Group #5**.
- If you have someone who has not led the group so far, let them lead this session. If all have led, let a volunteer take leadership.

Village Group #5

GATHER:

1. What need (or injustice) in your neighborhood just drives you crazy? Why?

FINDING OUR STORIES IN THE STORY:

John 13:1–17 (MSG)

[1] Just before the Passover Feast, Jesus knew that the time had come to leave this world to go to the Father. Having loved his dear companions, he continued to love them right to the end. [2] It was suppertime. The Devil by now had Judas, son of Simon the Iscariot, firmly in his grip, all set for the betrayal.
[3] Jesus knew that the Father had put him in complete charge of everything, that he came from God and was on his way back to God. [4] So he got up from the supper table, set aside his robe, and put on an apron. [5] Then he poured water into a basin and began to wash the feet of the disciples, drying them with his apron.
[6] When he got to Simon Peter, Peter said, "Master, you wash my feet?"
[7] Jesus answered, "You don't understand now what I'm doing, but it will be clear enough to you later."
[8] Peter persisted, "You're not going to wash my feet—ever!"
Jesus said, "If I don›t wash you, you can't be part of what I'm doing."
[9] "Master!" said Peter. "Not only my feet, then. Wash my hands! Wash my head!"
[10] Jesus said, "If you've had a bath in the morning, you only need your feet washed now and you're clean from head to toe. My concern, you understand, is holiness, not hygiene. So now you're clean. But not every one of you." [11] (He knew who was betraying him. That's why he said, "Not every one of you.") [12] After he had finished washing their feet, he took his robe, put it back on, and went back to his place at the table.
Then he said, "Do you understand what I have done to you? [13] You address me as 'Teacher' and 'Master,' and rightly so. That is what I am. [14] So if I, the Master and Teacher, washed your feet, you must now wash each other's feet. [15] I've laid down a pattern for you. What I've done, you do. [16] I'm only pointing out the obvious. A servant is not ranked above his master; an employee doesn't give orders to the employer. [17] If you understand what I'm telling you, act like it—and live a blessed life."

2. How do you think Jesus must have felt when he realized that no one was going to wash his dirty feet?

Calling Servant Leaders

3. Read vs. 3–4 again. How do you think Jesus' "self-understanding" helped him make the decision to act?
   c. He wanted to show an object lesson
   d. He grabbed a teachable moment
   e. Other _____

4. Which person in the 'picture' do you most identify with? Why?
   a. Jesus—seeing the need and filling it
   b. Peter—slow to start but then jumping in headfirst
   c. Non-mentioned disciples—staying in the background
   d. Judas—waiting for the right moment to exit
   e. Other _____

5. When was the last time you felt like a real "foot-washer"? What was the most rewarding part of doing it?

ACCOUNTABILITY and CARING:

6. What might God want to say to you through this passage of Scripture? What kind of foot-washing might God be calling you to do, in the next two weeks?

8. How can this group best pray for you and hold you accountable to follow through on God's call?

WE SERVE (OUR MISSION):

_____
_____
_____
_____
_____

WE PRAY:

Pray for one another around your group silently, then let the leader close aloud.

CHAPTER 5 - GROWING GREAT GROUPS

Whether you're guiding an administrative board, a sports-bar Bible study, a music team, or something in between, every small group needs *greenness.*

Imagine *green* for a moment.

What flavor do you taste?

What pictures pops before your eyes?

Green is what happens when a group becomes a community of people who grow in healthy relationships—with one another—with God—with their world. *Green* evidences health and life.

But groups don't just turn *green* with a little pixie dust or wishful thinking, though a little pixie dust never hurts. It takes intentional, specific steps to facilitate the process, in partnership with God's Holy Spirit.

This chapter will guide through practical steps that are adaptable to most any group setting. The guidelines are set primarily in the context of leading a *Basic* Village Group, gathered in a home setting. Then further interpretations are added for other types of groups.

You will make adjustments for your group, in your setting.

FROM THE CLASSICS

"In reality, most churches already have some small groups. They may not realize it, but they are there. The groups might take the shape of a Sunday school class or a music group, etc. Still they are a small group; carrying out many good functions. You must begin to identify them and then get on with the task of starting new ones."[1]
—Carl George

1 This is from Carl George's seminal book *Preparing Your Church for the Future* (New York: Fleming Revell, 1991). Carl is one of the giants in the church growth and small groups movements. Contact him at: http://www. carlgeorge@metachurch.com or check out books at: http:// www.atlasbooks.com/marktplc/01930.htm#order.

GETTING PERSPECTIVE

Looking backward before moving forward keeps us from getting run over. It also gives us a fuller perspective of where we've been.

There is nothing new about the idea of small groups. Living in small groups or communities is as old as forever. As we said a couple of chapters earlier, the original Village Group was the Holy Trinity: Father, Son, Holy Spirit.

You'll remember that we described the first man and first woman as the *group* created in the image of the Trinity—a model for how all humans are to live and an analogy for the Church in relation to Jesus.

When Jesus traveled the earth, he never did it alone. He was surrounded by his close group of three, a larger group of 12, and others who supported him throughout his three years of public ministry. You may remember that his Village Group (and the generations to follow) were the focus of his prayer in John 15–17. He prayed that all who followed would live in unity—would know the community that he and his Father knew.

In addition, Church history is permeated with models of small communities that carried on God's Village Group design. From Acts 2:42 (where the newest believers met in home groups), slipping through the final pages of the New Testament, and into the multiple generations that followed, small communities gathered to affirm, support, and launch into ministry.

Wherever and whenever the Church has been vitally alive, there has always been a form of Village Groups at the core.

JOHN WESLEY

From my theological heritage, John Wesley may be the most important historical guide. He founded an entire movement on a set of groups designed to meet specific needs. Burning outside-the-walls of the Anglican Church, the group movement became the Methodist denominations in the United States.

Wesley's most important group was the *Class Meeting* where

the majority of believers met to grow as Jesus followers. The goal was for disciples' behavior to become more like that of Jesus.

The *Bands* were homogeneous groups by gender, age, and marital status. They were places of high accountability and deep honesty. The goal was to bring about transformation of motives.

The *Select Society* was for leadership training. Groups of women and men were equipped to lead groups and other ministries.

Finally, the *Penitent Band* was a place where people found the opportunity for restoration from addictions and other life struggles. This is similar to groups like Alcoholics Anonymous.

CONTEMPORARY GROUPS

The resurgence of the small group movement has been profound in the last 100 years. Some groups formed as places where people could discover vital faith in Jesus—something lacking in the week-to-week attendance of their denominational congregations. Others found congregational settings to be a frightening place to share struggles, or attempt to belong.

Along the way, *giants*—original dreamers—saw the need and led the way in this small group explosion. The rest of us have built upon their foundation.

Let me point to the four who are among the most important.

SAM SHOEMAKER

An Anglican priest in New York City and Pittsburgh, Sam Shoemaker was grounded in the Oxford Movement in England and founded the *Faith at Work* ministry. He is famous for what he called the "30-day experiment" for people living on the streets. He would offer, "Try Jesus for 30 days and if your life is not changed you can give him back."

BILL WILSON

Bill Wilson attended Sam Shoemaker's Oxford Group, searching for ways to meet the needs of alcoholics. Using Sam Shoemaker's ideas and mentoring, he founded Alcoholics Anonymous. Millions of people have been rescued and transformed through the powerful AA ministry and its offshoots.

LYMAN COLEMAN

Another person who created his groups on the shoulders of Sam and Bill, was Lyman Coleman. As described earlier, he is a powerful, personal mentor. He is the *small-group grandfather* of all who have worked with or created small groups since the 1960s, even if you've never heard his name. His founding of Serendipity House became *THE* resource for small group study guides, training seminars, and the Serendipity Bible. Thousands of individuals and congregations have been impacted.

Near our turn into the 21st century, after the death of his amazing wife Margaret, Lyman retired and sold Serendipity House. While processing his own grief, he discovered huge spiritual and personal needs among men, and began creating *man-tools*. Since then *Marked Men for Christ, One Year to Live,* and *Men of Iron* have seen thousands of men begin an adventure with Jesus. A new ministry to women (*Women of Iron*) is just getting started as I write these words.

One of the most impactful contributions of Lyman's ministry is his Relational Bible Study method—teaching us how to walk into the biblical story with a small group of friends, and discover Jesus in new and fresh ways.

ROBERTA HESTENES

For more than 40 years of ministry, Roberta Hestenes has pioneered in the small group movement. Her *Using the Bible in Groups* is a primary classic. From her leadership as a college president, a scholar, and pastor, her voice has resonated across the small-group landscape.

So as we create Village Groups, we're don't start from scratch. We build on an eternal plan that's been expressed in a kaleidoscope of forms throughout the centuries. And we build on a foundation laid by amazing people who've dared to show the way.

BACK TO GREEN!

Yep, I'm stuck on green!

Green is the color of dreamers. It expresses vitality and richness.

Green lights up the right side of our brains with images of growing things.

Now, imagine every current group in your ministry as *green*— becoming a healthy, growing place.

So, before you start adding new groups, plan to begin molding your current groups into a *greener* shape.

Ponder that idea for a moment.

If you're committed to make Village Groups the atmosphere your congregation breathes, then every group that currently exists in your ministry setting, needs to become a place where—

People's needs are cared for,

People grow as disciples of Jesus,

People serve in ministry to the church, their neighbors and the world.

(Sitting on a board should never be a person's primary ministry. That's an additional job that someone must do to keep an organization alive. Although, I'd suggest that you let some groups and administrative work just die.)

BETTER THAN DEVOTIONS

If you're like most church groups, you normally "have devotions" at the beginning of each meeting. This often consists of someone reading from a devotional book (or a few verses from the Bible) then offering to "have a quick prayer."

And so it goes. Each time the group meets, there's a little *God-thing* before the start of the important business.

But what would happen if your administrative board became a growing group where people's needs were cared for, where people grew more like Jesus, and where group members served in ministry beyond the board meetings? What if you had no more turf wars? What would you do with the extra meeting time if people were living deeply into one another's lives?

THERE'S A DIFFERENCE IN GROUPS

Throughout this book, as we've discussed a relationally-focused Bible study group—the Village Group—you may have wondered why I seem to have ignored other kinds of small groups. Certainly, there are nearly as many different *kinds* of groups, as *there are* groups. I see four basic models from which all other groups blossom.

- *Bible Study Groups* form because people want to study the Bible in a *deeper* way. They focus on learning content and Bible memory. They usually get into studying word orders and doing comparison studies between the Old and New Testament. Their biggest desire is to "know the Word."
- *Covenant Groups* focus on accountability between the group members. Members meet regularly to talk about how they have lived, what they've done wrong, what's gone right, and how they can do better.
- *Recovery Groups* target specific life issues such as addiction, divorce, or grief. Once they've formed, they are usually closed to new members, and meet for a specified number of times as set out by a curriculum.
- *Topical Groups,* like Recovery Groups, work with specific content but study various topics such as parenting, or last week's sermon.

While all of these groups have specific and good purposes, each group by itself, falls short.

In other words, if we begin one of the groups listed above, and do not include the broader aspects of the Village Group, we miss the point.

For example, if we fail to include the relational pieces of intentionally building a community, the group will never grow people who become more like Jesus. They'll not learn to apply what they're taking into their minds. And head-knowledge is never sufficient.

And if we fail to include service/mission we'll quickly become stagnant and never reach our neighborhoods and the world.

DOING GROUP BADLY

One group I coached kept coming back to me each week, telling me that they wanted to "go deeper" in Bible study. They didn't really think they should spend time on the "relationship stuff" I had created for them to do.

So each week they met and looked at biblical passages and delved into meanings of specific words. They did comparison studies in both the Old and New Testaments. They looked up the original Greek and Hebrew. This pattern continued for nine months.

As the school year concluded, one of the young couples who had been most enthusiastic about "deeper Bible study" announced to the group that they were leaving their marriage, getting divorced, and going their own ways.

Everyone in the group was shocked! They were astounded that this could happen! Why didn't they know this was coming?

Although sickening, it's the natural result of focusing on learning content while never taking time to live into one another's stories. Never taking time to build deep relationships of care. Never studying the Scripture in the context of a group life, so it becomes applicable to everyday situations.

The group had learned volumes of content but never learned life in community, where the three stories connect and the Holy Spirit brings transformation.

Jeff Kern gets it. "We confuse depth with muddy. We believe that if things are hard to understand they must be from God.

Instead the most profound ideas are simple."[1]

BUILDING A THREE-LEGGED GREEN GROUP

Think of a Village Group like a three-legged stool. Even if you've never milked a cow, it makes sense that we need all three legs to stay vertical. The same is true for Village Groups.

LEG ONE: RELATIONSHIP BUILDING

The first leg of the stool is building healthy relationships between group members. Here are four beginning steps to healthy relationships.

❖ *BE INTENTIONAL*

Healthy groups never happen accidentally. They are the result of sharing joys and needs, of praying together, and maybe most importantly, affirming one another.

❖ *BEGIN CASUALLY*

A great way to start a group meeting is with a *Gathering* question[2] that is indirectly related to whatever you'll be studying during the Village Group time. Standing[3] in the kitchen of a home, around a coffee pot, will help to warm up the group.

It's important, particularly for introverts, that people have something in their hands so they don't struggle to find pockets to put them in. A beverage or *light* snack works well. That's why cocktail parties are so effective in connecting people together.

A quick note! Unless you're having a party, don't pro-

---

1 Jeff Kern is the Organizational Development Pastor at Summit Church in Orlando, FL. He's a leader developer. Check out their website and amazing ministries at www.summitconnect.org.
2 This is one of several terms that is fully developed in LEG TWO.
3 Never provide enough chairs for everyone to sit down at the outset. It's preferable for everyone to stand until you move to the *Finding Our Stories in the Story* time.

vide large portions of food. The point is a snack, not a meal. If a snack is provided, cut the items into at least four pieces. People can always take seconds but you'll have much less waste, and thank me later.

Again, smaller is better.

For the first group meeting you'll probably want to start with a party to help people get acquainted. A *Gathering* question, tossed into the evening, can get the group thinking about future gatherings, and begin the telling of stories between group members.

❖ GREET NEW PEOPLE[4]

As the group leader, you are the best one to *open* the group to new people. People don't want to appear cliquish toward newcomers. They are shy and need someone to affirm that the new person is *safe*. You can open the old circle to new people by meeting them at the door, walking with them to the group, and introducing them around. Make sure to stay close until they are engaged in good conversation.

❖ SUBDIVIDE THE GROUP

When a group gets larger than SEVEN people, it's important to subdivide the group for at least part of your Village Group time. You will notice that when a group gets larger than seven, about half of the group joins in discussion while the other half observes.

The following suggestions may help make subdividing easier. As the leader, you will need to decide what works best for your people.

- THE ENTIRE GROUP can meet together for the *Gathering* question, a drink, and some food. Again you won't need

---

4 Check out Hugh Halter's book *Flesh: Bringing the Incarnation Down to Earth* (David C. Cook, 2014) for more great ideas.

chairs since people are standing around a coffee pot or barbecue grill.

- TWOS are good for interviews, for deep sharing and prayer.
- FOURS or FIVES are the best grouping for getting acquainted, for Bible study and discussion, for giving affirmation. Try to avoid groups of 3, which require a higher level of attention that can be exhausting. FOURS help everyone to participate.
- You may want to stay in FOURS for the time of *Accountability and Caring.*[5]
- The *We Serve*[6] commitments may be declared in the FOURS group or the ENTIRE GROUP.
- You may want to bring everyone together again for prayer, so the whole group can be aware of issues that the whole group should know about.
- Groups of EIGHT or more are great for worship celebrations, singing, and prayer if not everyone needs to talk. You can ask for *hot* issues to celebrate or pray for. If you find that the discussion goes too long, you may need to subdivide the next time.
- When you subdivide the group, make sure to give time signals (at least at the 5-minute and 2-minute mark) for when conversation must be cut off—for the next section of the meeting to begin.

While it's important to always be planning for the Village Group to birth new groups, subdividing allows a group to grow to almost any size, whether it's ready to birth or not. This would be particularly important if a group grows large very quickly, before an apprentice leader is ready to lead the group.

---

5 These are group-meeting section names that you've seen in the Turbo Group at the end of each chapter. You will find a complete description of each section later in this chapter.

6 Again, further explanation to follow.

LEG TWO: RELATIONAL BIBLE STUDY

Whenever a group meets together, we must assume that there are people with little or no biblical knowledge. Remember Wrestler Ron? Your people may not have lived Wrestler Ron's life, but many, if not most, have little biblical or church background. So we must level the *playing field* to make sure that all are equals, all have the chance to belong.

❖ *LEVELING THE PLAYING FIELD DEPENDS ON:*

▷ The Three-story principle.
As we described earlier, **three stories** must connect.
• The first story is God's story (primarily told through the Bible). That story shows God's design and creation of humans, documents our walking apart from God's plan, and explains God's becoming human to offer us a way home.
• The second story is another person's life story, with all its stuff.
• The third story is my story, with all of my stuff.

Remember Jesus' words about what happens when two or three people gather in his name.[7] So, we can count on it. When the three stories come together in a group of Jesus followers, amazing things happen.

▷ Using Narratives.
It's easiest for people to connect their story to God's story if the Bible passage they are studying is actually a story, not some theological section like a letter from Paul. It's possible to use a non-narrative section of the Bible as a compliment to the narrative, or at a time when the entire group has more

7 See Matthew 18:20.

experience with Bible study. However, if new people join the group on a particular week, you will need to jump back into a narrative passage so the playing field is level for the new person.

▷ Using the Right Questions.
The right *kinds* of questions and the *order* of questions is vitally important.

Questions must be open-ended, never fill-in-the-blank with a *correct* answer. No one should need previous biblical knowledge to answer any questions that come up in a group time. If you get into more difficult passages of study, you may need to get help from a resource person or book. But that's the exception, not the place to begin.

When you see our examples, some questions may appear needless if we were just teaching Bible content. But they are vital for building biblical relationships. And there is a specific sequence to the questions.

You may use Bible-study guides designed around this model or you can grab a Bible passage and do the same thing yourself.

However, a word of caution! **Writing *great* questions is hard work.**

So, when you decide to start writing your own material, gather a couple of other people who can edit and re-edit the questions until you get the best ones possible. We've given you a Question Guideline at end of the book.

❖ *THE RELATIONAL BIBLE-STUDY MODEL*

Now let's put the pieces together. Here are the specific parts of a Relational Bible Study that will work in your Village Group.

Relational Bible Study is built on the basic assumption that...

- We need to tell our story, connect that story to other humans' stories, and connect to God's story.
- All of us have an *inner child* who wants to be released. The best questions start by tapping into that *inner child*. Most everyone has a childhood story to tell. So when possible, tie questions back to ages 7–10 years of age. People with a troubled childhood may have difficulty answering some questions, but most will find it helpful because there is a distance between the past and the present group setting.
- We can "come to Jesus as a little child." So prepare to laugh and cry!
- This is NOT a place to teach the Bible as a cognitive activity, filling peoples' heads with memorized content. Instead, as we tell our stories in the biblical context, the scriptures will come alive and transformation will happen!
- Using Inductive Bible study techniques, people can walk into the scripture and dance around in the context—viewing the scenes from all angles.

So now as you read through the following outline that describes the Village Group session, remember that the questions are strategically worded and placed where they are to help the Three Stories connect around the Bible passage.

GATHERING (USUALLY THE ENTIRE GROUP TOGETHER):

The **GATHERING** question(s) is to get the group thinking about the biblical topic in a non-threatening way; often producing laughter, bringing out positive endorphins and reducing barriers to the deeper questions that are coming.

You may want to "toss" this question to the group, standing around a coffee pot in the kitchen. After a few minutes, send groups of four to various locations for the Bible study.

REMINDER: Get something into each person's hand at the beginning of your gathering. People, especially us introverts, will talk more openly if our hands are occupied, holding a mug or glass.

FINDING OUR STORIES IN THE STORY (BEST IN 4S OR 5S)

The group of four will read through the Bible passage together, preferably out loud.

The 2 or 3 questions right after the Bible reading help people put themselves into the scripture passage. This is where *inductive* Bible study really starts.

The next set of questions is to help the group *dig out some of the content.* You may want to add more here, but do it carefully so you don't bog the group down or lose sight of the overall purpose.

The looming temptation is always to *go deeper* in study by learning facts instead of letting the Bible touch our whole beings.

Finally, a set of *personal application* questions encourage a response to the scripture. The responses may range from superficial to profound and life transforming. As a leader, carefully affirm all responses as the group members' answers become more and more transparent.

As you demonstrate respect for all comments, you are modeling respect to your group members.

ACCOUNTABILITY AND CARING

(MAY BE DONE IN 4S OR ALL TOGETHER):

Accountability should never become a negative word. It pulls everything together. It shouldn't signify some authoritarian person demanding obedience from people. Instead, group members commit to stand together, to support each person's next step, and work toward the deeper health of the group.

During this time, group members will share life joys and

NOTE: The Village Group is designed to last 1½ hours. As the leader of the group, you know your group. And since you now know the *purpose* of the various questions, feel free to rewrite or adapt them. if discussion goes long on particular questions, don't panic, just cut somewhere else. However, as you adapt, *make sure to pick and choose from each type of question*, keeping them in the correct sequence. You will need about 8–10 good questions for a 90-minute meeting.

concerns, and you will have the opportunity to guide the group in *pastoring* one another.

WE SERVE (OUR MISSION) (4S OR ENTIRE GROUP TOGETHER):

Each session should include opportunity for group members to declare a commitment to serve (*go on mission*) in their community. It might be something as simple as introducing themselves to the grocery cashier. Or paying special attention to a neighbor. Group members should be especially aware of the *invisible people* in their lives, those they pass every day.

At the following meeting, each group member will report the results of their *mission*.

The serving assignment is usually related to the topic of the Bible study. This helps build a pattern of personal ministry for each group member.

At least every month or two, your group will want to find a way to serve together in your community, your city, or the world.

WE PRAY (4S OR ENTIRE GROUP TOGETHER):

After sharing joys, concerns, and plans for service, the group will join together to pray for one another. In the process, you will guide the group through various patterns of prayer.

In the section "Praying Together" (below), you'll find tools to help you introduce prayer to the group, and to help them begin praying aloud.

❖ READING THE BIBLE

Being called on to read aloud will strike terror into most any person, especially one with reading difficulties. These guidelines help prepare your group to read the Bible passages together, even if you've subdivided into fours for the Bible study time.

- Unless you know a person really well—and their reading ability—never call on a person to read *cold turkey*. This is especially true when reading the Bible, which can have difficult-to-pronounce names and complicated language structures.
- The best way to prepare a person to read is by pre-heating them before the session starts. Give them the opportunity to review the passage and plan for any difficult words or phrases.
- If a person volunteers to read but then has difficulty getting through a passage, feel free to assist them by giving them a word or two and letting them attempt to continue.
- Thank and compliment readers, particularly when the passage or pronunciations have been difficult.

❖ PRAYING TOGETHER

The quickest way to make your group members go spit-less, is to ask them to pray aloud. If you want to actually teach them to pray, try out these various forms of prayer, in a progressive way.

As you work through these four levels of prayer, you will decide when your group members are ready to move from one level to the next, at several-week intervals.

• **Level 1: You pray out loud.** As you model praying for the group, forget using special words or phrases you might have heard. (That's what scares people out of feeling competent to pray.) Just be yourself conversing with God.

• **Level 2: Specific prayers for specific needs.** After needs have been shared, ask for volunteers to pray for each need. Encourage the group to pray one-sentence prayers for the specific request, then stop. They don't need to say, "Amen." Instead they can simply say, "I'm done."
   For example: "Will someone please pray for John and Mary as they try to find a new refrigerator?"
   If no one volunteers, after giving a brief pause, you can again pray.

• **Level 3: Open-ended prayer by two or three.** Without designating anyone, say, "Let's have **two or three** group members pray before I offer a closing prayer."
   Don't be afraid of silence for a moment or two as group members decide if they will be one of those volunteers. If no one prays after a lengthy time (30 seconds or so) of silence, go ahead and pray out loud.

• **Level 4:** Ask the group to sit or stand in a circle and pray out loud around the circle by saying something like,
   "Dear God, this is _____. Thank you for _____. Amen."
   If anyone is uncomfortable, they can pray silently when their turn comes and just say "Amen" to let the next person know that they are done.

If your group is comfortable with touching, you might make a huddle or hold hands for the prayer.

Try variations on any of these prayer levels, such as having the group pray silently around the circle for the person on their left.

Or, ask subgroups to pray together, with the above guidelines. This will help the really timid person learn to pray aloud. You might walk from one subgroup to another, and guide them through the steps above.

Before long, most group members will be easily praying for one another. They just have to discover that it's safe to say what they're really thinking and feeling without the pressure to produce some form of *magic* words for God.

FROM THE CLASSICS
The Quaker Questions for Groups

These questions (or a variation) have been used for many years, in many groups. They help people learn to tell their stories in relaxed and easy ways.

1. Where did you live between the ages of seven and 12?

2. How was your house heated at that age?

3. What was the center of warmth in your home (a person, a stove, a special room)?

4. When in your life, if ever, did God become more than just a word?

LEG THREE: FINDING A MISSION

❖ *ON MISSION*

Alan Hirsch reminds us, "The church doesn't have a mission. God's mission has a church."[8] In other words, God's plan is to fulfill God's work through us.

Jesus came on God's mission.

Jesus' followers (God's Church) are called to that same mission/ministry.

As a goal, each person should be serving someone, somewhere each week. When we mature as disciples, we begin to understand that we are all in ministry, all the time, all our lives.

As described in the *WE SERVE* section, you, as leader, will encourage group members to declare a plan for serving between each time the group meets. Using a resource like MGames[9] will help the group members move from observers *of* mission to participants *in* mission.

Remember that the entire group should also serve together. That's easier to accomplish if group members live fairly close to one another. Try to create a serving opportunity with your neighbors once a month. Then once a month serve your city or the world. Particularly look for opportunities to partner with agencies or groups who are making a positive difference in your area—whether Christian-based or not.

In fact, if you partner with a non-church-based agency you will be amazed at how you impact the agency's members while serving their constituency group. Since Christians are generally known for what they oppose, the agency's members will usually not expect *religious people* to care about the

---

8 Alan taught a public session at VERGE\13, Austin, TX, March 27–28, 2013. He also has written on this subject in several places. Check out the resource section at the end of this book.

9 This great tool, created by Alex McManus, can be purchased at www.theimm. org (The International Mentoring Network). It's a creative way to get your group started living missionally.

environment, the poor, or people outside the church walls.

And your serving time must never be a time for judgmentalism or preaching.

Just SERVE!

❖ THE EMPTY CHAIR

A starting mission for all group members comes in the form of an empty chair. Each group member will constantly be on the lookout for friends and neighbors to fill the empty chair—to join your Village Group.

It is important to plant the idea of MISSION or SERVICE at the very first gathering of the group, then reinforce it each time the group meets.

❖ MAKING BABIES

A third form of mission for every Village Group is birthing new groups.

My best small group learning experience was also the most painful. I split up a group of 30 people into three groups of 10. As a small group ministry *expert* I thought I knew how groups must be done. I walked into a new congregational setting and told the group leader that we needed two more leaders, to start two more groups. He willingly followed my direction.

What you need to know is that the group had been subdividing in their meetings for many months. The group was full of life and vigor. They had a strong identity as a growing group of 30+ people. They really, really liked being together.

We had a birthday party for the two new groups. We interviewed the group leaders before the entire congregation. We launched the groups with great fanfare, a birthday cake, and a newspaper article.

Yet, within two months, two of the groups died.

People stopped attending. They had lost identity with the

larger group.

At the expense of this great group, I learned the hard truth between *splitting* and *birthing* groups.

How it's done is most important.

Groups don't usually birth a new group during the first 12 months of a Village Group's life. However, if they continue to 18 months, a birth should usually happen quickly.

From the first group gathering, plant the seed of a dream to birth at some future date, approximately 12–18 months out. Get the group used to the idea of *pregnancy*.

Obviously this won't work with an elected board, but it can with almost any other group in your ministry setting.

Though failures do happen, a few simple steps will increase the odds of a healthy and safe birth. It's better to get it right the first time than try to start over after a hard failure.

Birthing is the healthy creation of new group out of an original group. Never talk about *splitting* a group.

Once a group reaches 10 to 12 people[10], the group needs to start planning the birth. However, birthing should never surprise anyone. If we regularly discuss birthing from the beginning, it will be natural and expected when the birth-time comes.

Every group must have a group Apprentice as well as a Leader. When birthing a new group, the **original Leader** leaves to start the new group, with **three to six** volunteers from the original group. The **original Apprentice** stays behind to lead the original group. Both groups should already have new Apprentice Leaders ready to start when the birth is done.

The easiest way to birth a new group may be for the current leader to collect an affinity group (for example, parents of

---

10 If you're leading a ministry team, you'll need to decide how large you need to be to birth a new group. For example, if you're leading a worship band, then you can start duplicating instrumental positions immediately when you have new interested people. Once you get enough duplicate people to create a new band, do it.

2-year-olds). Those three to six people will invite others to join them. They might even start the new group studying something about parenting toddlers, in addition to their regular Village Group material. Within a few weeks they will return to their regular Relational Bible study.

Studying *only* the *affinity-topic* will get tiring quickly.

Birthing is easier if the original group and the newly-birthed group create a celebration party for the launch. You also might consider periodic "family reunion" parties with the original group to help all group members process the *birthing grief.*

Everyone is responsible for recruiting new group members to fill the vacancies (remember the empty chair) created by the birth—and to help grow the newly-birthed group.

Three legs keep stools stable.

Three legs grow Village Groups into healthy communities.

THOUGHT PROVOKERS (for individual reflection):

1. What big idea from this chapter just turns on your imagination or sparks a dream in your heart?
2. What are you going to do in response to that dream?

_____

3. Without looking back at the chapter, summarize the Three-Legged Stool model. What are some of the key points of each leg?

Leg One:

Leg Two:

Leg Three:

4. Now go back go back and see what key points you forgot.
5. This is an intense chapter for leaders to try to digest.
   What TWO issues from this chapter most leave you wondering
   or feeling like you need more help?
   a.

   b.

   Who will you ask for help?

   _____

   When are you going to do it? (Be specific.)

   _____

TURBO GROUP:

- Work through **Village Group #6.**
- Continue to pass the group leadership around at each ses-
  sion. Everyone should be sharing equally in leading the Turbo
  Group.
- Make sure to keep up with your **WE SERVE** missions each
  week. Then report back to the Turbo Group members.

Village Group #6

GATHERING:

1. If you had the chance to clean up one big mess in YOUR world (home, church, school, personal life) what would it be?

FINDING OUR STORIES IN THE STORY:

Mark 11:12–19 (TNIV)

[12]The next day as they were leaving Bethany, Jesus was hungry. [13] Seeing in the distance a fig tree in leaf, he went to find out if it had any fruit. When he reached it, he found nothing but leaves, because it was not the season for figs. [14] Then he said to the tree, "May no one ever eat fruit from you again." And his disciples heard him say it.

[15] On reaching Jerusalem, Jesus entered the temple courts and began driving out those who were buying and selling there. He overturned the tables of the money changers and the benches of those selling doves, [16] and would not allow anyone to carry merchandise through the temple courts. [17] And as he taught them, he said, "Is it not written: 'My house will be called a house of prayer for all nations'? But you have made it 'a den of robbers.'"

[18] The chief priests and the teachers of the law heard this and began looking for a way to kill him, for they feared him, because the whole crowd was amazed at his teaching.

[19] When evening came, Jesus and his disciples went out of the city.

2. Put yourself in the shoes of a disciple. How would you have re-sponded to Jesus "clearing" the temple?
    a. Ducked behind a pillar.
    b. Cheered him on from the sidelines.
    c. Helped him throw some tables over.
    d. Other _____

3. If you had been reporting for Jerusalem Cable News that day, who would you have most wanted to interview from this entire story— Bethany to Jerusalem and back? Why?

4. What do you think Jesus' actions, both toward the fig tree and the temple, tell you about Jesus' style of leadership?
    a. He was a hot-head.
    b. He willingly took on injustice.

    c.   He could stay focused on the most important things, even in a crisis.

    d.   He wasn't much of a servant leader.

    e.   Other _____

5.   How are you able to act as a servant leader in your actions when facing a frustrating or unjust situation? Or can you?

ACCOUNTABILITY and CARING:

6.   How might God be calling you to take a new direction right now? In what area of your life?

7.   During this next week, how can this group best hold you accountable?

    a.   Check with me on Facebook.

    b.   Call me twice.

    c.   Pray for me.

    d.   Meet me for coffee.

    e.   Other _____

WE SERVE (OUR MISSION):

_____

_____

_____

_____

_____

WE PRAY:

After those who want to report out have shared, let two or three people pray out loud for the group members.

FROM THE CLASSICS

8 THEOLOGICAL ASSUMPTIONS
BEHIND ALL VILLAGE GROUPS

YOU are created in the image of God and endowed with unlimited potential.

Your POTENTIAL can best be realized through Jesus Christ, in the company of a supportive Christian community.

To become a truly SUPPORTIVE CHRISTIAN COMMUNITY, you need to get to know one another in depth…and this takes time, effort, and a common commitment to life together.

Personal GROWTH begins with inner change as you respond to the invitation of God for newness of life.

The HOLY SPIRIT has endowed you with SPIRITUAL GIFTS for ministry to others—within your supportive community and through the community to the church at large.

SCRIPTURE is the living account of God's redemptive activity and the best guide for his will for right now.

Spiritual WHOLENESS includes your whole being— your emotions, your relationships, your values, and your lifestyle.

CELEBRATION happens naturally and spontaneously when you are set free in a supportive Christian community to discover and express the beautiful person you are in Christ.

—Lyman Coleman, *Encyclopedia of Serendipity*
    (Littleton, CO: Serendipity, 1976), p. 23.

CHAPTER 6 - THE TOP 8 Q&A

Are you ready for some Q & A?

Here are the eight most common questions I'm asked.

You'll notice that I've included questions and responses for both individual group leaders and people who wish to start a multiple-Village-Group ministry. So some will apply to you. Maybe some won't.

For example, if you're currently an individual group leader you probably won't have questions about coaching multiple groups. However, in the future, you may become an overseer where coaching is vital. So, if a question seems irrelevant for your particular situation, just skim the answer and place a memory-marker for later reference. You may come back to it if your situation changes.

Here is the TOP-8-questions countdown.[1]

---

1 I have purposely duplicated some responses, if they apply to more than one question. That way you only need to read the questions that deal with your issues of interest.

NUMBER 8—DOES IT MATTER WHERE WE MEET?

In a word, "Yes!" Various types of groups need different settings to be most effective.

Any time Village Groups prepare to start there's a great deal of discussion about where. Add these guidelines to your discussion.

❖ **Basic Village Groups**…
may meet in a home setting. If you decide to use a house, follow very carefully the guidelines in Chapter Five about starting and stopping on time.

Yet, the best choice is meeting in a *Third Place*[2] like Starbucks or a sports bar. Certainly, finding enough table space and working with the noise level can be troublesome, but worth the effort.

Before you decide, consider three reasons why a *Third Place* is better than a home setting.

- It's a *safe* place for group members to connect with people who have no church or faith connection. We've had people walk up to our table, ask what we are doing and want to join the group. If the group gets too large for a normal table setting, sub-divide or use a separate dining room.
- The group gets the chance to bless the owner and server of the *Third Place* by purchasing food and providing **really great tips**. If you're not willing to give over-the-top tips (at least 20%), please go back to someone's house. It's a terrible witness for Jesus to under-tip a server, whether they serve well or not. The group must see themselves as God's instruments of blessing to the server, not consumers waiting to be pampered.
- The *Third Place* meetings become a model for how a normal life of serving ministry is done. Getting to know the names of the managers and regular workers, finding out about their lives and their needs, and praying with

2   If you're not familiar with the term, *Third Place* references a place where people gather other than at home (1st place) or work (2nd place).

(and for) those workers becomes a group ministry. When the opportunity arises to meet one of the worker's needs, it doesn't fall to one person. The whole group is involved, and whoever is available can meet the need.

If a long-term need arises, the group members can rotate turns in ministering to the worker.

❖ **Recovery Groups...**

a special type of Village Group, generally should meet in an *institutional* or *neutral* type setting such as a church, a bank community room, or a recreation center. People who are walking through crisis in their lives are skittish enough when attending a group, so they need a place that feels secure and anonymous.

Meeting in a home feels unsafe to a person unsure of what is going to happen once the front door is closed. They will feel trapped. A neutral site allows for an easier opportunity to leave, if a person gets too embarrassed or too fearful to continue.

However, if you meet in a public location, try to find a secluded door for the group members to enter through. Again the goal is to feel secure, anonymous, and confidential.

❖ **Ministry Teams...**

a variation of the Village Group, and will usually meet where they do their work. Changing up the location, like going to a *Third Place* can be a helpfully-creative way to improve group life.

If you're working with a board, a lawn crew, usher team, etc. they usually get used to meeting in the same place, and have specific seats they repeatedly use. Changing the location can change the group dynamics. As you begin to *green up* the group, go slowly in making location changes as well. Most board members are very traditional and change of any sort is difficult.

If your group is a music or worship leadership team, it's wise to change the venue for the *group-time*. If the group meets where the rehearsal is held, the setting (like the instruments) will cause tension between doing the group work and rehearsal. This is where "out of sight, out of mind" can be helpful.

NUMBER 7—HOW OFTEN SHOULD WE MEET?

First, group gatherings must become central for those who are committed to growing more like Jesus. Life in the Village Group is the life-atmosphere for a congregation, a top priority for the individual members.

Dare I say, if a choice must be made between the Village Group gatherings and the weekend worship events, the Village Group should take precedence. That is not to say that the worship events are not vital. Both the Village Group and congregational worship are extremely important and should rarely conflict if people are willing to make difficult schedule decisions.

❖ **Basic Village Groups**...

should meet EVERY week for at least the first SIX weeks. This allows the group to get used to one another's *warts*.

Warts are those different views of life that we each carry.

And we could never imagine sharing life with someone who really thinks that different than us.

By the end of six weeks, group members discover that those *warts*—those differences—are what bring dynamic richness to the group. If the group doesn't meet each week during those early days, they may never work through the *warts*, and the warts will become divisive, until someone leaves the group.

Continuing to meet every week is the best plan.

However, after the first six weeks it is possible to switch to a modified every-other-week meeting model. Never go to an actual "every-other-week" plan. Since some months have a fifth week, people will get confused and miss gatherings, and begin to disengage. Rather, choose specific days of the month such as the first and third Tuesdays of each month.

However, the IDEAL monthly schedule would look something like this. You can adapt it to fit your group and its specific needs.

- Meet 2 or 3 weeks for Bible Study and sharing group life.
- Meet 1 week to serve in the neighborhood

- Meet 1 week to serve the city or world

Those **serving weeks** may include a brief time of Bible study and prayer together, depending on what the serving ministry looks like, and how long it takes.

❖ **Recovery Groups...**

will normally meet every week. The group members need consistent support of the members. They will usually close the group to new members by the second week and remain closed for several weeks. They then re-open to add new members. Many groups such as *Divorce Care* use a specific curriculum that dictates the group structure and number of meetings in each series—usually about **eight** weeks.

Some recovery groups are required by their charter to remain open continuously. They would obviously follow those guidelines.

❖ **Ministry Teams...**

usually find it more difficult to arrange group meetings, since most do not meet weekly. Some groups like ushers may have never meet together. So this will be a brand new concept to them. Note the comments on how long to hold a meeting, in the next section.

The rule of thumb for ministry teams:

Meet when and as often as you can—whenever the group normally meets.

Groups like worship leadership teams, who meet every week, should do some group work every time they meet.

NUMBER 6—WHAT ARE THE SEASONS OF A GROUP LIFE?

Village Groups, may continue together indefinitely; however, just as there are calendarized seasons, groups have life seasons. In other words, don't be discouraged if you sense the need to take a break from one another.

Your local school calendar makes a good, over-arching, nine-month season. Inside of that there are shorter seasons.

As discussed above, the first six weeks are the work-through-the-warts time. Most of the emphasis in those initial six weeks is building healthy relationships with some Bible study and some missional focus.

As the group evolves into the next number of weeks, less time is usually needed for building relationships as the focus moves strongly into fulfilling the group and individual mission. As mission grows, so will healthy relationships.

Depending on the Village Group's mission, holidays may become times for a brief break. The same may be true during summer with periodic *check-ins*, parties or missions.. The regular schedule would begin again with the start of the school year.

A Village Group should plan to birth another group by about 12-18 months. This boosts group vitality and expands the group mission.

At some point, the group may decide that they've been together, with this particular set of group members, for long enough. There are various reasons for this. Sometimes it's because the group didn't add new members, didn't birth a new group, or boredom has set in with the group's particular personalities, etc.

Don't panic—be honest.

Evaluate the reason for your desire to shut down the group, so you can learn from the experience.

Then THROW A PARTY!!!!

Celebrate the time you've had together as a Village Group.

Give one another tokens that you'll keep the rest of your life, to symbolize the wonder of your friendships. Then bless one another and move on.

REMEMBER, Village Groups are how the Jesus-life is done, so reconfigure or join other existing groups, and get on with your ministries.

NUMBER 5—SHOULD WE HAVE OPEN OR CLOSED GROUPS?

One group I knew named themselves "The Disciples."

You can guess why they chose the name.

There were 12 group members and no one else was welcome. That's not a Village Group, or any kind of healthy group. Instead that's a stagnant group of people who become bitter, gossiping, and unwilling to serve those outside their little circle.

Open groups are those that are always looking for new members and welcome any and all who come. *Closed* groups either don't like new people or have a specific reason to *close* for a limited and specific time period.

Let me build off the comments in the last sections, with some further explanation.

❖ **Basic Village Groups...**
should always remain open for new people. The empty chair and the group's mission demand openness. By using questions that level the playing field (as we described earlier), everyone can tell a piece of their story, and new people can be quickly incorporated into the group. It doesn't take long for new members to catch-up with the stories of the longer-term members.

❖ **Recovery Groups...**
may be both *open and closed*.

As mentioned earlier, many groups use a curriculum or have a charter that defines the *open* and *closed* policy.

If there is no policy, a good plan is for the group to remain open for two sessions, allowing new members to join. Then they *close* the group for a specific time, to allow for deeper confidentiality. After the specified number of meetings (again, no more than eight) the group *opens* again for new members to join.

❖ **Ministry Teams...**
can be a bit tricky.

For elected groups or boards, the groups are automatically closed to new people until the next election. I'll not get into the political issues of trying to get *new blood* elected in a congregation. To say the least, it can be volatile! You may need to live with what is, and look for health in other areas.

Other forms of ministry teams should always remain *open* to new people as a way of multiplying their ministries. Some teams have an audition process or requirements for membership, but all should have a chance to apply.

If every ministry team saw themselves as *open* there would probably never be a shortage of people for any ministry.

Every group member would be looking for someone who could replace themselves and birth another group.

NUMBER 4—WHAT SORTS OF RESOURCES ARE ALLOWED?

First, let me say, start a group by using some sort of Study Guide that uses the Village Group model to get you into the Bible—99%-100% of the options you'll find at bookstores DON'T. So shop carefully.[3]

Since most USAmericans (especially Christians) have grown up with the idea that we learn by *information dumping*, it is **unnatural** for us to lead relational Bible study groups.

Once you understand, and have practiced leading and writing questions with a Guide, you can use the Bible itself and create your own questions and discussion tools.

Throughout this book we've discussed the importance of forming healthy relationships around the discussion of a Bible passage. Then we talked about leveling the "playing field" by using the right kinds of questions and letting each person contribute their own story.

The quickest way to stop group growth is to show up with authoritative books like Bible commentaries or textbooks. When a question is asked, there may be some discussion but people will always look to whoever is holding the commentary for the *official right* answer.

---

3 We would love for you to use the resources we've created just for these purposes—to get people intentionally building healthy relationships with God and one another through Relational Bible study. If you're interested, check them out at the end of the book or at www.DonQDox.org.

The same paralysis happens when a pastor or Bible professor shows up for a group session. A few group members will hesitantly answer the question, then all heads will pivot toward the expert—who, if wise, will not answer the question. "Professional" Christians must be careful in how they contribute to a Village Group or they will kill it by becoming the expert on all things biblical.

In Village Groups, there are no right or pat answers. That doesn't mean we never want to know what the Bible says for sure. But remember, all understanding of scripture comes through our personal lenses of interpretation. There is no such thing as the *official* biblical answer. When a person says, "I just follow the Bible," they mean that they're following their interpretation of the Bible, whether they know it or not.

So, what do you do if someone presents some really off-the-wall (obviously unbiblical) response?

First, thank them for the answer and their willingness to share it. Then suggest that there might be another answer, as the group looks further into the Bible.

Obviously, the goal of the group is not to just share ignorance. But if people are stifled in giving their opinions, they will shut down. People will think they are too dumb or feel embarrassed to say what they're really thinking.

"Consider this: All Christians (Jesus-followers) affirm the creeds. Everything else is personal opinion and not worthy of division."
— Steve Harper, founding vice president of Asbury Theological Seminary–Florida Dunnam Campus, retired professor and pastor.

It is okay to allow for differences of opinion as long as they are argued respectfully. The goal is for each person, in the context of the community, to discover how to grow more like Jesus. Often that means wrestling with tough issues, maybe never agreeing, but loving one another just the same.

If you run into a particularly difficult topic with lots of disagreement, it might be helpful to ask a person with some biblical training to meet with the group, to offer their insights.

However, remember that their insights are just that, that person's informed opinion.

3—HOW DO WE AVOID THE MEETING TIME-TRAP?

First rule of group life: ALWAYS START AND STOP ON TIME! Period.

Remember, if you don't start on time with those who showed up, the group will catch your pattern and continue to arrive late. If group members know that they'll miss something if they don't arrive on time, they'll put out the effort to arrive promptly.

If some group members are consistently late, ask about their schedule. Are there work issues? Is there a specific traffic problem? The group may need to adjust the starting time to meet the late-arrivers' needs.

And, if the group runs past the announced closing time by more than five minutes, stop the group. Announce that the meeting is over and anyone who wants to stay longer may do so. (You may also need to announce a maximum time to stay for those who have no restraint.) This gives people who must leave the freedom to depart. When groups run past the announced closing time, people will not return. They will feel *taken advantage of* and trapped.

The length of meetings depends on the group and any curriculum that the group uses. Let me suggest that 1½ hours is a great length. Longer sessions get tedious very quickly, unless there is a group agreed-upon reason to extend the time.

Adapt the following basic example for your setting.

❖ **Basic Village Groups...**
- Total Group time: 1½ hours
- **Gathering**: 10–15 minutes (whole group)
- **Finding Our Stories in the Story**: 20–30 minutes (in 4s)
- **Accountability and Caring**: 10–15 minutes (whole group or 4s)
- **We Serve**: 10–15 minutes (whole group or 4s)
- **We Pray**: 10–15 minutes (whole group)

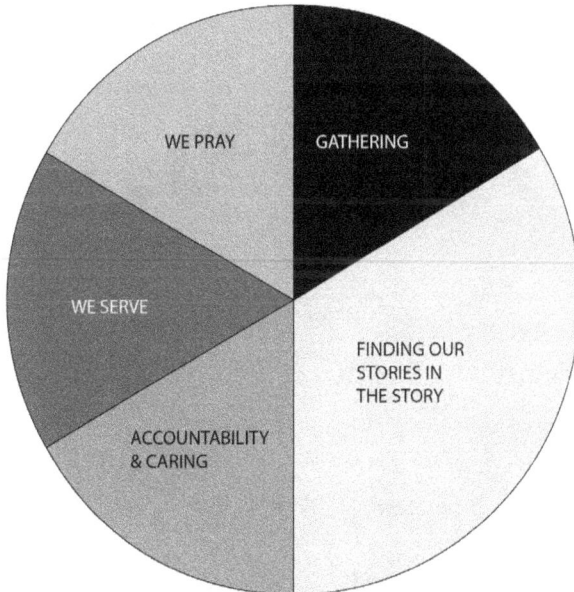

❖ **Ministry Team...**
- Your total meeting time will probably exceed 90 minutes. However, if you start with the "group time" before the business agenda, you'll find that the business will usually get done more quickly and you'll still be completed on time.
- Your board or ministry team will probably combine the **Gathering**, **Finding Our Stories in the Story**, and **Accountability and Caring** sections. You may reduce the time to about 30 minutes total.
- The rehearsal or business work will be an expanded **We Serve** time.
- You may then close with **We Pray**. Don't cut the prayer time short by filling the time with too much business and talking.

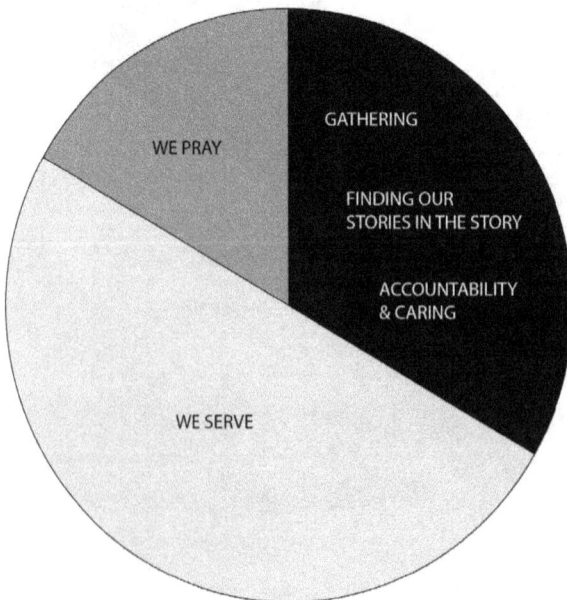

NUMBER 2—HOW DO WE GET NEW LEADERS?

The simple answer: GROW them.[4]

Apprentices

First, never start a group without an Apprentice leader. The Apprentice will share leadership of the group as part of the Group Leader's mentoring process. The entire group aids in the mentoring by affirming the Apprentice.

Whenever the group is ready to birth a new group, the Apprentice will stay with the original group and the original Group Leader will take a few volunteers as a core, to start the new group.

We've learned over the years that sending an Apprentice to start a new group is almost always a failure. Apprentices blossom best in their original group.

Rising Apprentices

Rising Apprentices are people who have no idea that they might someday be a group leader. However, as you observe them in various settings, you'll note that they have leadership potential. When you sense the time is right, you'll encourage them to become an Apprentice. If they agree, they can become an additional Apprentice in the original group or become the Apprentice when a new group is birthed out of the original.

Coaching

Mentoring or coaching, as we've discussed earlier, is vital for group health, and growth of new leaders.

A coach should be a successful current or past Group Leader. Don't recruit coaches who have never successfully led a Village Group. Inexperienced coaches do not understand the Village Group purpose or the issues that arise in groups. Plus, they have

---

4 Carl George, master church consultant for many years, is the originator of many of these ideas about group Apprentices, Rising Apprentices, Coaching, and Coaching inventories. Check out his website at: carlgeorge@metachurch.com. His ministry wisdom has impacted thousands of us.

no validity with other group leaders.

Coaches should be assigned to FOUR or FIVE group leaders. The coach will meet with each Group Leader individually, for about **one hour** per month. Your sharp mind has already figured out that this breaks down to about one hour of coaching per week.

Most anyone can schedule an additional hour into their week.

The point of coaching is to give guidance and encouragement to the Group Leaders. You will want to use some sort of form[5] for the coaching interviews—to keep records of what you discuss, and how each group and leader is progressing.

In addition, all group leaders and coaches should meet together once a month (or at the least once every other month) for training, nurture, and encouragement. Leader meetings should be a story-packed hour and one-half, to discuss struggles and celebrate victories.

AND NUMBER 1—HOW DO WE DEAL WITH DIFFICULT PEOPLE?

People always come first, and treating them gracefully is *priority ONE.*

That said, there are some situations where the only way people can be cared for gracefully is through a firm-loving word. They require *Extra Care.*

Setting up guidelines for the group **at the very beginning** will give you a tool for reminding group members of what is expected in group sessions. In fact, printing a list of group guidelines that everyone agrees to, can be most beneficial. I'm not talking about a list of stifling rules, but some general group guidelines.

Here are SIX examples.

Confidentiality is *over-the-top* important. If a person breaks confidence with something that is said in the group, it can destroy

5 Look in the Resource Section for a sample Coaching Interview Form.

the person who originally shared the information, and it may destroy the group. Once trust is lost, it's nearly impossible to regain.

The only way a confidence *may be broken* is if someone shares information that suggests they may hurt themselves or someone else. In such a case, the Group Leader must tell the person who revealed the information, "It's not safe for the group to maintain this confidence, and the proper authorities will be notified."

People must NOT **confess another person's *sins*.** People are only allowed to talk about their own issues. Couples tend to be notorious for this. They will tell on their spouses. Or workers will report on their co-workers or boss. You will need to interrupt an overly disclosing person to remind them of the guideline.

If a person truly needs to share a difficult situation, such as abuse, they should probably do so with only a portion of the group. Then the group can help the person seek professional help and safety.

Prayer-Gossip will kill a group. Some groups become *hot houses* for gossip. Watch for comments (or prayer requests) that are actually cloaked gossip.

If an individual dominates the conversation with their own struggles—in more than one meeting—you will need to talk directly to that person. Privately alert them to the fact that the group cannot carry all they keep *giving*.

It may be necessary to ask a person to either not keep *unloading* on the group or actually leave the group. A Village Group cannot provide therapy. That takes special care from a professional. And it is dangerous for a group to attempt to help a person who needs professional care. If a person "unloads" in only one specific meeting, the leader will need to decide whether to recommend professional help or not. The leader would be wise to seek professional assistance from a counselor, before recommending a referral.

Advice giving is not appropriate in a group. Advice is cheap and not usually helpful. In a Village Group, we support one another, but we won't try to give answers unless asked for. Even when a person asks for advice it must be given in small doses. Most people who request advice are not really seeking it. They are seeking a listening ear to help them talk through their issue.

Conversation dominators will dampen group life. If a person regularly dominates the group discussion, the Group Leader will need to meet the person in private to discuss the situation. The person may not realize what they are doing.

Sometimes, placing the dominator next to the Group Leader, where the Group Leader can put a hand on the person's shoulder when they interrupt, will solve the problem. The group leader may need to interrupt the dominator by saying something like, "Bill, let's hear from someone else, now."

That's plenty to think about but certainly not all the questions that will arise as you lead a Village Group or coach a series of groups.

But you don't need all the answers to get started.

When other questions arise, review the chapters you've just read to remind yourself of the basic principles for Village Group life…and charge on!

THOUGHT PROVOKERS (for individual reflection):

1. Here are a few key words to keep in the front of your mind as you begin or continue leading a Village Group. Take a few minutes to write a summary statement, from memory, about each, then go back and compare with your reading.

    Community

    Three-legged stool

    Relational Bible Study

Coaching

Rising Apprentices

Servant Leadership

Importance of the right questions

Leveling the Playing Field

Wrestler Ron

Think "Green"

Subdivide the group

Group service/mission

Birthing the group

Levels of Prayer

TURBO GROUP:

- You've been working through this book, as a group. It's time to get started with leading your groups—recruiting a few people to join you in this great adventure. If you're already leading a group, you've hopefully learned a few insights to make your Village Group even *greener*.
  But first, complete one final wrap-up session—**Village Group #7**. You'll affirm what y'all have been processing together— and commission one another into the future ministry God is guiding you toward.
- Pray and ask God for a BIG DREAM! Then take the risky next-steps—following God into fulfilling that dream.

Village Group #7

GATHERING:

1. If your group hired an artist to create a sand sculpture that demon-
    strates your most intense passion, what would the sculpture look like?

    Take 2 minutes to draw a sketch, then go around the group, each
    person describing their "passionate" sculpture design.

FINDING OUR STORIES IN THE STORY:

1 Peter 2:4–10 (MSG)

[4] Welcome to the living Stone, the source of life. The workmen took one look
and threw it out; God set it in the place of honor. [5] Present yourselves as building
stones for the construction of a sanctuary vibrant with life, in which you'll serve
as holy priests offering Christ-approved lives up to God. [6] The Scriptures provide
precedent:
    Look! I'm setting a stone in Zion,
    a cornerstone in the place of honor.
    Whoever trusts in this stone as a foundation
    will never have cause to regret it.
[7] To you who trust him, he's a Stone to be proud of, but to those who refuse to
trust him,
    The stone the workmen threw out
    is now the chief foundation stone.
[8] For the untrusting it's
    a stone to trip over,
    a boulder blocking the way.
    They trip and fall because they refuse to obey, just as predicted.
[9] But you are the ones chosen by God, chosen for the high calling of priestly
work, chosen to be a holy people, God's instruments to do his work and speak
out for him, to tell others of the night-and-day difference he made for you— [10]
from nothing to something, from rejected to accepted.
[11] Friends, this world is not your home, so don't make yourselves cozy in it. Don't
indulge your ego at the expense of your soul. [12] Live an exemplary life among
the natives so that your actions will refute their prejudices. Then they'll be won
over to God's side and be there to join in the celebration when he arrives.

2. If your life had never been encountered by Jesus "from nothing to
    something, from rejected to accepted" (v10), where do you think
    you would be right now?

3. What does it mean to you, to be considered a "building stone for the construction of a sanctuary vibrant with life?"
   a. finally proves I'm a hard head   b. gives my life purpose
   c. I'm part of something really big   d. means I'm really valuable
   e. other _____

4. What is the most important way that God has used you this month as a priest to others?
   a. caring for kids   b. pastoral care stuff   c. with a friend
   d. on the Frisbee golf course   e. other _____

ACCOUNTABLE and CARING:

5. Affirmation is one of the greatest acts of priesthood that we can offer to others. We all need to give it; we all need to receive it.

   • Go around your group, one at a time.
   • Put one person (they may not respond, just receive) on the "hot-seat" then the other group members share a brief affirmation statement about that person.
   • When all the group members have given their affirmation statement for the "hot-seat" person, one person pray a prayer of blessing and commissioning for what God wants to do in and through that person in the coming days.
   • Then go on to the second person. Continue to each person, until all have been affirmed, blessed and commissioned.

WE SERVE (OUR MISSION):

Decide how each group member will continue a life on mission. Will you continue to report in to another group member? Make sure when you start your new Village Group, to immediately get the group members into serving missions.

WE PRAY:

If you can, create a group huddle.
Each person pray silently for the person on their right.
Ask one person to give a blessing over the group before you depart.

AFTERWORD

AS A VILLAGE GROUP LEADER...

"Engage yourself in the process. Don't just observe.
Let Christ center the group.

Tell your own story. Emphasize experience over analysis.

Listen with your heart. Receive feelings and facts as given.
Judge not.

Model by doing. Be vulnerable, open, affirming.

Give no advice!

Share time equally.

Honor the right to pass.

Practice confidentiality. Keep stories contained in the group.

Exercise your power to bless! Call forth one another's gifts.

Be accountable for your own growth.

We care; Christ cures. Pray for one another."[1]

---

1 By Doug Wysockey-Johnson, from Lumunos, P.O. Box 307, Marlborough. NH 03455-0307, www.lumunos.org

RESOURCES AND COACHING

STAY FRESH

We've been resourced by many people, books and materials from many places. We've also created some resources that might be helpful. You'll find the following in this section:

- How to contact us.
- *Third Place* resources we've created that will get you started in outside-the-congregational setting groups.
- Books that have helped us in our ministry.
- A sample *Coaching Form* to guide you in creating your own.
- A *Question-writing Guide* to help you create your own great discussion questions.
- *The Apostle's Creed* and *The Nicene Creed*

❖ CONTACT THE AUTHOR

Email: Daryl.Smith@asburyseminary.edu
or dlcbsmith@gmail.com
Website: DonQDox.org

❖ THIRD-PLACE RESOURCES FOR YOUR
VILLAGE GROUP [guides to get you started]

The Gathering Place Series: a 4-book, outside-the walls small group resource.
[Order from **www.wifpandstock.com** or Amazon.com]

Overloaded: *keeping it together when you're stressed to the max!* by Daryl Smith (Wipf & Stock, 2013) 62p.
ISBN:978-1620329122

Discovering Faith by David Solano (Wipf & Stock, 2013) 52p.
ISBN:978-1620329146

Jesus: the man behind the stories by Daryl Smith (Wipf & Stock, 2013) 72p. **ISBN:978-1620329139**

God in Story by Brian Babcock, Patricia Clarke, Carolyn Smith, James H. Sullivan (Wipf & Stock, 2013) 70p.
ISBN:9781105681295

❖ A GUIDE FOR BEGINNING JESUS FOLLOWERS

Radical Journey: a 20-week discipling immersion with Jesus in the Sermon on the Mount by Brian Babcock, Curt Deming, Carolyn Smith & Daryl Smith (order at **www.Lulu.com**, 2013). Each week includes: ENGAGE—personal study; VILLAGE GROUP; EMERGE—serving/mission resources.

❖ BOOKS & SITES WE'VE GROWN FROM

[This is a partial list to get you started. Read anything written by these authors, and you'll be well served.]

Alan & Deb Hirsch

Website #1: **www.ForgeAmerica.com**
Website #2: **www.Sentralized.com**

Untamed: reactivating a missional form of discipleship by Alan & Debra Hirsch (Shapevine, Baker Books, 2010)

The Forgotten Ways by Alan Hirsch with Darryn Altclass (Brazos Press, 2009).

The Permanent Revolution by Alan Hirsch & Tim Catchim (Jossey-Bass, 2012).

Fast Forward to Mission by Alan Hirsch & Lance Ford (Baker Books, ebooks edition, 2014).

Redeeming Sex: Naked Conversations About Sexuality and Spirituality by Debra Hirsch (Forge Partnership Books, 2015)

Jen & Brandon Hatmaker

Barefoot Church: serving the least in a consumer culture by Brandon Hatmaker (Zondervan, 2011).

Interrupted: When Jesus Wrecks Your Comfortable Christianity by Jen Hatmaker (NavPress, 2014)

7: An Experimental Mutiny Against Excess by Jen Hatmaker (B & H Books, 2012)

Hugh Halter & Matt Smay

Website: **www.missio.us**

The Tangible Kingdom: creating incarnational community by Hugh Halter & Matt Smay (Jossey-Bass, 2008)

And: the gathered and scattered church by Hugh Halter & Matt Smay (Zondervan, 2010).

Flesh: bringing the incarnation down to earth; learning to be human like Jesus by Hugh Halter (David C. Cook, 2014)

Bi-Vo: a modern guide for bi-vocational saints by Hugh Halter (Missio Publishing, 2013).

Alex McManus
Makers of Fire: the spirituality of leading from the future by Alex McManus (IMN Idea Lab, 2014)

Rob & Kristen Bell

Velvet Elvis: repainting the Christian faith by Rob Bell (HarperOne, 2012)

Zimzum of Love by Rob & Kristen Bell (HarperCollins, 2014).

Reggie Mcneal

Missional Communities: the rise of the post-congregational church by Reggie McNeal (Jossey-Bass, 2011).

Present Future: six tough questions for the church by Reggie McNeal (Jossey-Bass, 2003).

Tony Dungee

The Mentor Leader (Tyndale House, 2010)

❖ SAMPLE COACH'S INTERVIEW FORM
for use with VILLAGE GROUP LEADERS[1]

Date: _____

Community Group Leader(s): _____

Interviewer: _____

As we start this, let me get a few details about your group.
1. Who is the group that you're leading?
2. How many meetings have you led this group since it started or birthed a new group?
3. When did your group meet most recently?
4. When did you last meet with your coach?

Now, let's talk about the life of the group.
5. What are some of the great things that are happening with people in your group?
6. What are some of the biggest struggles your people are facing?
7. Are there special needs or situations in your group where you'd like to have a Pastor's help?
8. What progress are you seeing in your Apprentice? How are you helping them develop?
9. What progress are you making in identifying Rising Apprentices? Who are you nurturing to become an Apprentice?

1. Adapted from Carl F. George in *Nine Keys to Effective Small Group Leadership*, 1997).

10. What are the best Bible study materials that you've used so far?
11. What stories are your group members sharing about carrying out their daily serving ministries?
    About opportunities to share their faith story?
12. What is your group doing to serve the neighborhood or the world?
    When is the next "event" you have planned?
    Who/What agency is your group partnering with regularly?
13. What new people are you and the group members approaching about joining your group?
14. When do you see a possible group birth time coming?
15. What help do you need to grow as a better leader?

Now to some specific details:
16. How many adults were present at your last meeting?
17. How many children are connected to your group?
    How are you caring for the babysitting needs?
18. How many of your regular group members are also regular worship attenders?
19. How many faith-explorers or guests were in your group meeting?
    a.   What did you do to put them at ease?
    b.   How did it work?
    c.   What might you do differently next time?

Finally, let's talk about caring for the people in your Village Group?
20. Do you have a regular prayer/care list for the group?
21. How many people are on your LIST (include regular attenders, occasional attenders, potential attenders)?
22. How many on your list are moving toward Jesus or made a profession of faith since the group started?
    Have any of them been baptized?
23. How many people on your list have you been in touch with between your last two meetings?
24. What resources do you need?
25. How can I best pray for you, right now?

Pray with the Community Group Leader(s)

• about their concerns,

• express thanks to God for them,

• and close with a blessing for their continuing ministry.

❖ SMALL GROUP QUESTION DESIGN GRID

The Basic Relational Model	Community Building	Additional Content/Creative Options	Comments
The Opening Question (1 or 2); A non-threatening, topical question or activity to engage the group in the study's topic; if possible, connect to the inner child.	We each tell our stories...		Ex. Draw an oval to represent your kitchen table at 7 years old. On this picture, draw in the "center of warmth" for the family (a person, pet, stove, etc.) OR Describe your high school "pecking order." Where did you fit?
Scripture Passage Use narrative story to "level playing field"		If no new members, the group may choose to cover the same topic with something other than narrative. Always be ready to "punt" back to narrative.	The use of narratives is preferred unless the group has an extended group life with no new members present.
The Connection Questions (2 or 3)	We each tell our stories in relation to God's story	Ex. Add a journaling suggestion or art project to express the story	Ex. If you had been Peter when Jesus was taken away, how would you have felt? What might you have done?
Content Questions (2 or 3); bridging from the "Emotional to the Application;" "What do I need to know in this passage?		This is the point to add more in-depth content questions with a group that has been together for an extended period, with no new members. OR This group may study specific additional biblical material related to their ministry team focus.	Ex. What do you think Jesus would want us to pay most attention to in the story of the prodigal son?
Personal Application (1 or 2); connecting my story to God's story.			Ex. If I were to take seriously what Jesus said here, I'd have to change (blank).
Accountable/Caring Community (1 or 2 questions)	Ex. From this time together, what is God asking you to do? How can this group help you be accountable to follow God' direction this week?		Teach the group through these accountability opportunities to carry deep pain with giving advice, and to walk through sensitive situations while keeping confidences.
Serve the World		Give examples for individuals. This is an area that the entire group should also do together, periodically.	Ex. What specific "action steps" will each person commit to take to make a difference in someone's life—in the neighborhood, city or world

Some Group QUESTION GUIDELINES:

- Use open-ended questions. No "Yes/No" responses allowed.
- Use as many multiple choice answer sets as reasonable.
- Connect questions to the "inner child" when possible—at least for the early questions.
- Make sure to include some "goofy" responses and an "other" in each set.
  Ex. How would you have felt if you had been in Peter's shoes when Jesus was taken away? a. Like a real dork; b. terrified; c. "Let me outta here!"; d. "What can I do to help?"; e. Other _____
- Always write questions that Wrestler Ron can answer without knowing the Bible or feeling embarrassed by the "biblical scholars" in the group. The questions should be safe for him to answer.
- Always level the playing field by making sure that each group member has opportunity to tell his or her story.
- Remember the "flying wedge" through the life-cylce of the group
- Use FOURS or FIVES for sub-dividing Bible study, avoid 3s.
- Ten questions should do it for a 1.5 hour meeting. Four or five questions should be needed for a 30 minute ministry team meeting.

❖ APOSTLES' CREED

I believe in God, the Father almighty,
creator of heaven and earth.

I believe in Jesus Christ, God's only Son, our Lord,
who was conceived by the Holy Spirit,
born of the Virgin Mary,
suffered under Pontius Pilate,
was crucified, died, and was buried;
he descended to the dead.
On the third day he rose again;
he ascended into heaven,
he is seated at the right hand of the Father,
and he will come again to judge the living and the dead.

I believe in the Holy Spirit,
the holy catholic church,
the communion of saints,
the forgiveness of sins,
the resurrection of the body,
and the life everlasting. AMEN.

❖ THE NICENE CREED

From: The Lutheran Book of Worship
The Book of Common Prayer (Episcopal)

We believe in one God,
the Father, the Almighty,
maker of heaven and earth,
of all that is, seen and unseen.

We believe in one Lord, Jesus Christ,
the only Son of God,
eternally begotten of the Father,
God from God, Light from Light,
true God from true God,
begotten, not made,
of one Being with the Father.
Through him all things were made.
For us and for our salvation
he came down from heaven:
by the power of the Holy Spirit
he became incarnate from the Virgin Mary,
and was made man.
For our sake he was crucified under Pontius Pilate;
he suffered death and was buried.
On the third day he rose again
in accordance with the Scriptures;
he ascended into heaven
and is seated at the right hand of the Father.
He will come again in glory to judge the living and the dead,
and his kingdom will have no end.

We believe in the Holy Spirit, the Lord, the giver of life,
who proceeds from the Father and the Son.
With the Father and the Son he is worshiped and glorified.
He has spoken through the Prophets.
We believe in one holy catholic and apostolic Church.
We acknowledge one baptism for the forgiveness of sins.
We look for the resurrection of the dead,
and the life of the world to come. Amen.

www.ingramcontent.com/pod-product-compliance
Lightning Source LLC
Chambersburg PA
CBHW021130020426
42331CB00005B/706